"Donna Dukes has a gift for beautiful words. Words that reach across political and social lines to touch people where they live, allowing them to imagine, on their best days, where we all might live. But it is not her words that inspire the most. It is not even the work she does to educate students who have run out of options. Dukes' inspiration is found in the love she gives teenagers who have been written off as unlovable. It is the smile she demands of herself when circumstances seem insurmountable. Donna Dukes is hope, where few others have the strength to maintain it. Somehow, she has become the hope for all of us."
—John Archibald, winner of the Pulitzer Prize 2018, winner of the Pulitzer Prize 2023, author of *Shaking the Gates of Hell: A Search for Family and Truth in the Wake of the Civil Rights Revolution*

"Important and extraordinary, *This Way to Hope* instantly draws readers into the disturbing, little-known world of critically at-risk students who face life and death struggles daily. A master storyteller, Dukes crafts an emotional yet non-saccharine narrative—rare in non-fiction writing—by weaving real-life student experiences within every chapter. These poignant examples enable readers to understand a complex issue and its human impact with an intimacy that spans despair and hope. The epitome of resilience and relentlessness, Donna Dukes illuminates a social justice challenge desperately in need of transformation."
—Andre P. Beaupre, author of *The Purposeful Nine*, Founder of Soulful Advantage

"I couldn't put it down! *This Way to Hope* is a phenomenal book! Maranathan Academy is an amazing school! And Donna Dukes is a woman everyone should know! *This Way to Hope* gives anyone truly interested in helping the underserved an opportunity to learn effective ways to make the most impact on the lives of critically at-risk students."
—LisaRaye McCoy, NAACP Image Award Nominee, Actress, Philanthropist, Humanitarian

"*This Way to Hope* explains how to reverse entitlement mindsets and help critically at-risk students achieve success. Readers will be inspired by the incredible way Donna Dukes has dedicated her life to giving second chances to students others have written off. Having hope is life changing!"
—Rickey Smiley, author of *Stand by Your Truth: And Then Run for Your Life!*, Nationally Syndicated Radio Host: *The Rickey Smiley Morning Show*, Comedian, Actor, Philanthropist, Humanitarian

"Educating and empowering youth who are critically at-risk is Donna Dukes' calling. She not only guides her students with hope, but she also serves as their anchor during the most difficult and unpredictable life events. In her book, Donna does an excellent job of relaying the truth of her students' experiences when they enter Maranathan Academy, along with the joy of their rediscovery of youth and unlocking of their potential. As many schools are cutting back on efforts toward health and well-being, Donna succeeds in creating a safe space which provides a wholistic approach to education, including lessons in leadership and opportunities for physical, emotional, and spiritual well-being and growth in addition to individualized core curriculum. Her passion, efforts, and vision truly make her a champion in the eyes of her students and her community."
—Heather Austin, Ph.D., Pediatric Psychologist

"Donna Dukes is truly inspirational. *This Way to Hope* is an amazing literary work showcasing her journey and unconditional love for her students. To give a critically at-risk student a second chance is one of the greatest gifts possible…Donna Dukes is helping her students choose education over incarceration."
—Michael Williams, Secret Service, Deputy Assistant Director (Retired), Washington, D.C., Kappa Alpha Psi Fraternity, Inc., National Deputy Director of Public Safety

"This is a book that needed to be written, and only Donna Dukes could write it. Now, everyone—especially teachers and others who work with critically at-risk youth and adults—needs to read it."
—Frank White, author of *The Overview Effect: Space Exploration and Human Evolution*

"Eye-opening, important book! These stories will challenge your understanding of a world where every day is a struggle for survival. *This Way to Hope* gives those who encounter students from that world tested tools to make a real and dramatic difference in their lives."
　—T. K. Thorne, award-winning author of *Behind the Magic Curtain: Secrets, Spies and Unsung White Allies of Birmingham's Civil Rights Days*

"*This Way to Hope* is a much-needed literary work for the African American community. It serves as a framework for societal leaders within oppressed communities to use to create internal systems of support to lift others as they climb."
　—Dr. Stevie Lawrence, II, Vice-President Postsecondary Education Southern Regional Education Board

"As an educator with more than four decades of experience, I have witnessed the intensification of debilitating circumstances faced by students of color from underserved communities. *This Way to Hope* provides a replicable model for helping critically at-risk students overcome those circumstances and enjoy bright futures."
　—Dr. Yvette M. Richardson, Ed.D., Ed.S., M.S., Alabama State Board of Education Representative, District 4

"*This Way to Hope* by Donna Dukes showcases the work of Maranathan Academy, which epitomizes what being a Kiwanian is all about—education, progress, and changing communities."
　—Keith McKendall, 2023–2024 Governor Kiwanis International Alabama District

"*This Way to Hope* is another brilliant effort by Donna Dukes to raise awareness and compel action with a poignant argument regarding the moral responsibility for the village to raise all children, no matter their circumstances."
　—Sheriff Mark Pettway, Jefferson County, Alabama

"*This Way to Hope* is a must-read for those in education and social work...gives us a glimpse of the incredible challenges that our most critically at-risk students face but, more importantly, a wonderful view of what these students can achieve when given the hope, encouragement, and support they need."
 —Dr. Gregory McLeod, President,
  Edgecombe Community College

"The work Donna Dukes does at Maranathan Academy makes it possible for individuals to receive an education, secure employment, leave a government assistance, and government housing. *This Way to Hope* shows others how she is able to attain outstanding results for individuals facing extremely challenging circumstances."
 —Armon Matthews, Director of Client Services,
  Housing Authority of the Birmingham District

"Donna Dukes has written a book that will impact the lives of young people for generations to come; it is insightful, concise, and full of life lessons learned by those whose lives she herself has impacted in the best of ways. This Way to Hope is an inspiring work meant to bring about the necessary change in the way our culture views critically at-risk students, the paths many of them are on, and how they can be guided toward achieving the most their lives can offer them. Donna is to be congratulated for having produced a publication that not only highlights Maranathan Academy and the wonderful work she and it does, but also in having created a school model that will surely encourage others to attempt the same effort in their communities. Thank you, Donna."
 —Wayne Coleman, Head of Archives,
  Birmingham Civil Rights Institute

"The work that Ms. Dukes does with critically at-risk students is life-changing! You cannot read this book without being moved."
 —Dr. Shurita Thomas-Tate, Missouri State University

"In the forgotten corners of our cities and towns, a crisis is unfolding. Millions of our most vulnerable citizens—children—are becoming part of the critically at-risk population caught in the vicious cycle of poverty, violence, hunger, and lack of opportunity, their hopes and dreams are being slowly extinguished. This Way to Hope is a path forward towards hope, education, and success. Donna Dukes takes readers on an inspiring journey into the lives of those being left behind, sharing their raw stories of struggle and resilience. However, this book is much more than simply raising awareness of the challenges they face.

Drawing from decades of hard-won experience, Dukes devises a clear, practical, and proven framework for transforming lives and communities through evidence-based programs in mentoring, education, job training, and community development, she demonstrates how the most at-risk individuals can reclaim their dignity and potential. Filled with uplifting real-life stories of personal transformation as well as inspiring accounts of community rejuvenation, This Way to Hope shows us that even in our most disadvantaged neighborhoods, great positive change is possible. For anyone who has felt hopeless about the injustices pervading our society, this book provides a powerful reminder that a better world is within reach—if we have the courage to build it, one valuable child at a time."
    —Dr. Rodney E. Harris,
    LCMHC-S, NCC, BCC, BC-TMH, ACS
    Associate Professor/Licensed Clinical Mental Health Counselor/Supervisor

"A book of successes and truths that transcends all eras and cultural boundaries is called *This Way to Hope*. This book is thought-provoking and will inspire you to want to help. CRITICALLY AT-RISK STUDENTS are seen by Donna Dukes."
    —Dr. Sharon J. Porterfield, Dean of Education,
    Stillman College

"A phenomenal guide with thought-provoking insight that unmasks the trauma today's youth face. Each story shows pure purpose, resilience, and a transparency that truly embraces hope. A must-read, especially for educators and anyone working with children from underserved communities."

—Arlinda Davis, Education & Ambassador United Trauma Informed Classroom, 2024 Winner—Shell Urban Science Educator Development Award of the National Science Teaching Association

"This Way to Hope is an instant classic, especially for those of us who share a concern for humanity. Donna Dukes' delivery is gritty and entertaining. Her compassion is nothing short of Christ-like."

—Dr. J. David Harris, MD

THIS WAY TO HOPE

THIS WAY TO HOPE

The Challenges, Hard Truths, and Triumphs of Working with Critically At-Risk Students*

*Juvenile Offenders • Endurers of Trauma, Poverty, and Neglect

DONNA DUKES

Published in the United States by Optimiste Publications LLC
This Way to Hope Copyright © 2024 by Donna Dukes.

All rights reserved. No portion of this book may be reproduced in any form without written permission from the publisher or author except in the case of brief quotations embodied in critical articles and reviews and as permitted by U.S. copyright law. This publication is designed to provide accurate and authoritative information in regard to the subject matter covered. While the publisher and author have used their best efforts in preparing this book, they make no representations or warranties concerning the accuracy or completeness of the book's contents. Neither the publisher nor the author shall be liable for any loss of profit or any other commercial damages, including but not limited to special, incidental, consequential, personal, or other damages. No part of this publication may be reproduced, distributed, or transmitted in any form or by any means, including photocopying, recording, or other electronic or mechanical methods, without the publisher's prior written permission, except as permitted by U.S. copyright law.

For speaking engagements or interviews with the author, as well as purchases in bulk for promotional, educational, or business use, please email requests@optimistepublications.com

www.optimistepublications.com

Print ISBN's: Hardback: 979-8-9898423-4-6
                Paperback: 979-8-9898423-1-5
Ebook ISBN: 979-8-9898423-5-3

Editors: Amy Pattee Colvin - Phase II
        T. K. Thorne - Phases I and III
Copy Editors: Chris Jones
               Village Editorial
Cover Design: Donna Dukes, 100 Covers, & Rocky Heights
             Print & Binding
First Edition: 2024

Dedication

To my fellow frontline workers in the critically at-risk world— teachers, social workers, law enforcement officers, health care providers, and more, for continuous dedication. We leave it all on the field—every day. Hang in there. It's worth it!

Inexpressible thanks to T. K. Thorne, my sensei in this effort. Thank you for believing in this book from day one, lending your genius, and sharing the light of your indomitable spirit. I wish words could convey the depth of my gratitude for your encouragement and limitless patience.

Contents

Prologue	xv
PART 1: The Critically At-Risk World	
Ch 1 What Is Critically At-Risk?	1
Ch 2 Critically At-Risk Students Need Us More	3
Ch 3 Trapped in the Critically At-Risk World	11
Ch 4 Working in the Critically At-Risk World	17
Ch 5 The Grey Zone	27
Ch 6 A Sneaky Form of Slavery: Government Assistance Dependency	33
Ch 7 Unintended Consequences	37
Ch 8 The CAW Journey	43
Ch 9 Scenes From a Parallel Universe	47
Ch 10 You May Now Enter the Whirlwind	53
PART 2: Cycle Breakers That Set the Stage for Success	
Ch 11 Getting the Backstory	59
Ch 12 Facilitating Chip Removal	63
Ch 13 Education and Encouragement	69
Ch 14 Nurturing	73
Ch 15 Dismantling Dangerous Mindsets	81
Ch 16 Providing Hope	85
Ch 17 Making It Safe to Dream	95
Ch 18 Sharing Uncomfortable Truths	99
Ch 19 Recognizing and Rooting for CAW Categories	111
Ch 20 Confronting the Unthinkable	121

PART 3: Essential Strategies for Successfully Working with Critically At-Risk Students

Ch 21 Defy the Entitlement Mindset	129
Ch 22 Take Nothing for Granted	137
Ch 23 Think Outside the Box	143
Ch 24 Require Improbable Peace	149
Ch 25 Fight the Stigma Against Mental Illness—Creatively	153
Ch 26 Understand the Importance of an Anchor Parent	163
Ch 27 Create a Team of Champions for a Child	175
Ch 28 Adopt a "Ride 'Til the Wheels Fall Off" Mindset	183
Ch 29 Accept the Fact that Sometimes You Will Lose	187
Ch 30 Remember Why You Serve	193
Ch 31 Watch for Hidden Toxicity in Good Homes	197
Ch 32 Access and Sympathy: The Importance of Setting Boundaries	205
Ch 33 Recharge, Reminisce, and Relish	213
Epilogue	217
References	219

Prologue

Grace

"If you feel comfortable, would you tell me about a crucial moment from your life, something that changed you?" I asked Grace, a newly enrolled student at Maranathan Academy.

Slowly, she straightened from a typical half-slouch student posture, plucked a lollipop from the jar on my desk, and then gave a far-from-typical reply.

"I was gang raped by five men when I was eight years old," she said in a flat, emotionless voice, then glanced to her right before adding, "and again when I was eleven."

Susan, a social worker from a local youth services agency, sat next to her in the chair normally occupied by a parent. She had called earlier that morning to brief me on Grace—whose rapists hadn't been caught—and request an emergency admission to Maranathan.

"Were any charges pressed?" I asked Grace, already knowing the answer but wanting to gauge how she felt about the status of her case.

"No, ma'am." She said quietly, her eyes empty and dark with sadness. Then she sat back and seemed to retreat into a world of her own.

I forced down my anger over criminals not having to answer for their crimes and focused on what was important—Grace, and bringing light into those empty eyes.

Wondering how to help her, my gaze strayed to a wall photo slated for use in a promotional poster for the school. Beneath the image of me with three smiling students, the caption would read, "Maranathan Academy, saving lives through the transformative power of education: one critically at-risk student at a time."

I glanced at Grace, then back at the photo, and suddenly remembered what had caused its featured students to succeed—hope and a chance to explore opportunities.

My gaze returned to Grace. "What do you want to be when you grow up?"

"A doctor," she said without hesitation.

The social worker and I smiled at her confident answer, and the three of us settled into a discussion on the course of study that would be offered, filled out a class schedule, and discussed available volunteer opportunities. There was no doubt that Grace would do well. She was bright. No, she was brilliant—a straight-A student with standardized test scores on the collegiate level in every subject. She was also six months pregnant with a boy she'd refused to consider putting up for adoption and had already named Joseph. The baby's father was nineteen years old and had disappeared as soon as he heard about the pregnancy.

Grace's mother, I later learned, was excited about the baby. Although this beautiful girl had off-the-charts intelligence and incredible collegiate potential, her pregnancy was the only time her mom had ever been excited about anything Grace did. She had been fourteen years old when she gave birth to Grace and living with relatives who viewed and treated children as useful burdens to supplement their meager income. So it wasn't the joy of a grandchild that fueled Grace's mom's excitement, but thoughts of what she could buy with the extra check a new baby would bring into the house.

Grace, however, was determined to be a good mother. Nestled between the textbooks in her book bag was a paperback on how to raise a boy. She was going to need all the parenting tips she could get, for none would come from her family. In the eyes of his grandmother-to-be, Joseph had already been reduced to a number—a dollar amount, a check, before he even took his first breath.

The assessment ended with an upbeat conversation on ways to navigate being a single mom while going to college and medical school. A support "village" to help Grace navigate her educational journey would be crucial. The road to college and medical school as a single mother promised to be especially long and challenging for Grace.

She was only twelve years old.

Welcome to the world of critically at-risk students—where being robbed of childhood is routine.

PART 1
Critically At-Risk World

Chapter One

What is Critically At-Risk?

The "at-risk" student category is relatively well known and usually assigned based on socioeconomic status, family composition, neighborhood crime rates, and so on. However, more than three decades of experience working with students of color from underserved communities has taught me that the at–risk category exists on a continuum, one I've found to be best served and understood via the creation of subcategories—good, fair, serious, and critical.

- **Good:** The student has an excellent support system consisting of at least one individual—parent, guardian, mentor—who believes in education, understands the importance of a strong work ethic, and consistently encourages the student to excel in school.
- **Fair:** The student's support system is moderately weak. The support system has a good work ethic and the belief in education, but stressors—job woes, economic hardship, health issues—usurp time and focus away from the student.
- **Serious:** The student has a weak support system comprised of an individual or individuals with little or no work ethic and only a slight belief in education. Lack of money, dysfunction among family members, and neighborhood crime result in the

student receiving only a scant amount of attention and almost no encouragement to pursue academic achievement. The family has a history of dependency on government assistance, and in some cases, the student's safety is uncertain.

- **Critical:** The student has a nonexistent or extremely weak support system consisting of an individual or individuals consistently unemployed. Education is not valued, and academic achievement is discouraged. The family has a history of incarceration and dependency on government assistance. The student often goes without food and other basic needs. If a support system is present, traumas such as severe bullying, sexual violation, or violent crime have affected the student to the extent that learning in a traditional school setting is difficult, if not impossible.

Students from the *critical* subcategory are the focus of my work. Each day, they encounter challenges that threaten their very survival, so much so that I coined a term: critically at-risk. The life circumstances of my students are far removed from what's considered "normal," and the decisions they make often seem counterintuitive or irrational to those outside of the critically at-risk world (CAW).

Many have parents or guardians who try to make them quit school to deal drugs, have babies, or turn tricks. Most live in situations so horrible that just surviving is iffy, and success is out of the question unless someone or something intervenes. Maranathan Academy—a nonprofit, private, alternative school located in Birmingham, Alabama—is that something.

Chapter Two

Critically At-Risk Students Need Us More

I founded Maranathan Academy and serve as its executive director and development officer. Supporters and interested onlookers frequently ask, "Why do you only take critically at-risk students?"

My answer is always the same, "Because they need us more."

Critically at-risk students need more time, encouragement, and attention than their traditional at-risk counterparts. At Maranathan, our students receive unconditional concern and patient guidance as they work to overcome circumstances that have stripped them of hope and rendered them unable to dream.

Many of our students suffer from feelings of abandonment and experience loneliness, even while living in a crowded household.

Maranathan gives them a chance to create a family when an alternative to the one they were born into is needed. It provides an environment where they are showered with love instead of abuse.

Edward

Edward placed a white carnation on her casket. Everyone else had started back to their cars as soon as the minister said, "Ashes to ashes, dust to dust . . . ." But not him.

Ready to depart, the other mourners began to yell to Edward, "Come on!"

He didn't move—couldn't move. He couldn't walk away and leave her there all alone. Walking away would mean this was real, that she was really gone—his angel and protector, his Aunt Ruth. Edward didn't want her to be gone, and he was afraid to leave her and the love she represented—the only real love he'd ever known. He had another reason not to walk away from her coffin. Doing so would require him to go live with the worst people he knew—his mother and her girlfriend. His two little brothers were already there. Thoughts of them, how young and defenseless they were, gave him the strength to leave Aunt Ruth's grave. As he walked to the waiting cars, Edward decided it would be his job to protect his brothers.

In spite of his maturity and noble aspirations, Edward needed a source of protection himself. He was only eight.

Six years later

"My auntie was real nice. She took me to church, and we used to cook all the time," Edward said. Now an eighth grader who'd been labeled "slow," he had recently been kicked out of a juvenile detention boot camp after being expelled from the Birmingham City School System for fights. One of the fights had been so violent that the student he'd fought had to be hospitalized.

According to the emailed interview request sent by his probation officer, Edward was ". . . going to be sent to real, adult jail the next time."

I agreed to meet with Edward and came face to face with an ominously quiet young man, a seething ball of barely controlled rage. Sensing pain behind the rage, I asked him to tell me about himself, which he did—honoring me with details that served to identify what was fueling his violence.

His facial expression was blank as he shared that his mother had given him to her Aunt Ruth when he was only a few weeks old. A big smile emerged as he talked about being raised by his aunt in what had obviously been a household filled with love. Later, when his biological mother gave birth to two more little boys, Aunt Ruth welcomed each into her housing community apartment—liberally dispersing love in place of any material things she may have lacked. Everything changed when she became ill with an aggressive form of cancer. The two younger boys went to live with their mother, but Edward stayed by Aunt Ruth's side until the very end.

When death came, it ripped him from the loving arms of the only mother he'd ever known, robbed him of a stable home, and sent him spiraling into an earthly version of hell—his biological mother's apartment.

In the early days of his enrollment at Maranathan Academy, I heard some students teasing Edward about sleeping outside. I called him to the office and asked if it was true. It was. He explained that his mom and her girlfriend, Platinum, told him daily that they couldn't "stand him." In fact, when Platinum got angry with him—which was often—she'd put him outside, lock the door, and make him sleep on the porch of their housing community apartment, no matter the weather. He had to fend for himself for food.

One morning, shortly after I learned this from Edward, his mother called to tell me he was in the hospital. The previous night, after being put out on the porch again, he had punched his fist through the front room window, cutting an artery in the process. He'd barely missed severing tendons.

His mom actually seemed baffled over Edward's actions. I didn't comment on her "confusion" and offered no sympathy. Self-destructive rage should have been an anticipated consequence of Edward being locked out of his own house—a house he knew was being supported by the Family Assistance Program (Welfare) money his mother received each month to help with his and his brothers' care.

Every time his mom let Platinum lock him out, Edward became enraged and thought about the clothes, weed, and booze the two women bought for themselves. Hunger pains throughout the night intensified his anger. He brooded over the fact that he and his brothers had nothing to eat except for the food they got at school—even though his mom received food stamps. His injury was the result of one lockout too many.

Anger had driven his bare fist through that window. When I spoke with him later that day, he verified what happened and the intensity of his anger, saying, "I was so mad. I didn't even feel it."

I explained to Edward's teachers that he would be absent for several days, detailing his injuries and how he got them. They were livid. Cries of "Call DHR!" rang out.

I reminded them that a few years before we met Edward, the Department of Human Resources (DHR) had taken the boys from the home. But, even though I thought there was little chance DHR would be able to intervene, I reached out anyway to Edward's current caseworker, Mrs. Williams, a stoically dedicated woman. She shared that Edward's case file chronicled the past neglect he and his two younger brothers, Dante and Mark, had suffered. She went on to detail the negligence, which ranged from failure to keep utilities on, uncleanliness regarding their clothes and bodies that was extreme enough to violate health department codes for safety, verbal abuse, and leaving the boys without adult supervision for days at a time. These incidents resulted in them being removed from the home on more than one occasion.

Just as I feared, the latest incident with Edward wasn't severe enough to warrant removal from the home or even an investigation because his injury, though provoked, was self-inflicted. She also explained that because DHR had taken the kids before, Edward's mom was a system veteran who'd learned to walk the line just enough to keep them from being taken again.

Sensing my frustration, Mrs. Williams encouraged me to remember that DHR focuses on keeping families together and family restoration. I understood what she was saying—barring Edward's mom killing her children or nearly killing them, she would probably always get them back.

My heart aches for caseworkers like Mrs. Williams. They have limited options and frequently struggle to help clients like Edward and his brothers. In cases where parents or guardians know how to work the system, DHR can offer little respite from "bad home environments."

What qualifies as a bad home environment? An incident from Edward's freshman year at Maranathan Academy gives a graphic example.

It occurred after school on a predictably sweltering August day. Edward made a surprise return just as the teachers and I were about to lock up. He explained that the city bus had broken down and would not be able to get him home. Sadly, this happens in some public transportation systems. I told Edward that I would take him home.

"No," said Adam, our math teacher. "I can take him home. I'm going that way."

I was hesitant to accept the offer. Adam had been brought up in a very affluent White community in Birmingham, and Edward lived in Birmingham's most violent housing project. "No," I said, "It's Gate City."

"I can do it!" Adam insisted, "Please let me take him home."

I refused again before finally agreeing—with misgivings.

They left, and about ten minutes later, I got a phone call from Adam. In a frantic, higher-than-normal voice, he blurted, "Donna, I'm on Edward's street, and police are everywhere!"

Unsurprised, I said, "Yeah, it's Gate City. That's why I told you to let me take him home. Can you get through?"

"No, Donna. Police are everywhere!"

"I understand that, Adam. It's Gate City."

"No! You don't understand. There's a body in the front yard!"

Still unsurprised, I said, "Okay, but can you get through?"

"No, Donna! The body is in Edward's front yard."

That got my attention. "Oh dear! Bring him back."

The body was Edward's favorite cousin. He'd been shot through the head by a friend during an argument. As the tenant, Edward's mother was held responsible for such a violent crime happening at her apartment. She was evicted. The victim's fiancée sought revenge by calling DHR, but again, the children weren't taken.

Edward's mother fought like a tigress to "keep her family together." The faculty and I observed her antics with a disgust borne from awareness that the boys went without basic things—unless we provided them. Despite his mother's vehement declarations of "love" for her children, what she really wanted were the checks they received each month. It was left to us to help Edward navigate his journey.

Accepting that DHR's limitations ruled out orchestrating a rescue for Edward and his brothers led me to explore and learn the art of unorthodox student aid. I decided to make friends with Platinum—Edward's mom's girlfriend—and open a dialog. After several conversations, she agreed to stop putting Edward outside. That victory allowed me to share some parenting and patience development techniques that made Edward's presence in the home more acceptable to her. Additionally, I regularly invited Platinum and Edward's mom to attend parent meetings and school events and to participate in our wrap-around services regarding career and college guidance and support. Platinum accepted my invitation and embarked on a career in hospitality. Edward's mom refused.

At school, I created customized tasks for Edward, which made him feel indispensable to the school's daily operations and motivated him to attend. Little by little, he began to trust, smile, and even laugh. Within two years, his eyes went from filled with anger to shining with confidence and hope. He became excited about the future, got a part-time job the moment he turned sixteen, and earned promotion after promotion.

Before we knew it, Edward was a high school senior and ready to graduate. During commencement week, we learned he would need transportation to the ceremony. His mother refused to come. So, I asked a Maranathan staff member to help me provide transportation for him and one of his brothers. It was a joy to watch him walk across the stage.

After graduation, he got a new job, moved into his own apartment, and began learning the trade of welding. Although the training will take longer due to his having to work full-time, Edward is happy and full of hope. He has broken his family's tradition of cyclical government dependency and is determined to help his little brothers break it, too.

He's off to a good start. His little brother, Dante, the only sibling to come to Edward's graduation, is now a Maranathan Academy graduate. During Dante's enrollment, a retired Air Force Colonel spoke to our students. Afterward, I asked each student to share what they had gained from hearing the Colonel talk. Dante's answer was just one word—Hope.

At my prompting, he explained that hearing about the military had shown him there was a path to get out of his neighborhood, learn a trade, and have a career. Hope. Recently, he graduated, and I had the joy of going to a military recruitment station to see him off to attend basic training. He is thriving and fully intends to make a career out of it. I'm so proud of him!

It gets better. Edward's mother went through a remarkable transformation. During his little brother Dante's junior year, she finally accepted my invitation for a career and needs assessment. Within six months, she was working part-time and exploring opportunities for community college, all while being encouraged by a support village consisting of her sons, me, and some Maranathan faculty members. Dante's commencement sported a sizeable, cheering entourage of family and friends. Guess who was cheering loudest? His mom!

Consistent nonjudgmental invitations and reminders gave her the courage to try for a better life. Though not completely free from dependency on government assistance, she's well on her way. Her sons and the Maranathan Academy support village couldn't be more excited.

Chapter Three

Trapped in the Critically At-Risk World

The critically at-risk world (CAW) can be likened to quicksand, that dangerous type of quagmire that lures people to their doom by appearing to be solid ground. Several times a year, organizations and government agencies provide CAW residents with special days of outreach events that yield clothes, toys, and gifts, as well as sumptuous luncheons and dinners. Such days, though needed, result in residents viewing the struggle-filled CAW culture as sustainable.

It is imperative to negate that view by way of the positive impact of education. Having the opportunity to attend school, experience horizon-broadening field trips, and meet persons whose lives contain only occasional struggles helps critically at-risk students become aware of a different style of living—that escaping the CAW is possible. Subsequently, critically at-risk students earn high school diplomas, pursue additional education, and ultimately become established in viable occupations that pave the way for them to enjoy lives outside of the CAW.

Founded in 1991, Maranathan Academy specializes in critically at-risk youth and adult students, providing them with a multifaceted education in an inclusive, nurturing, non-judgmental environment, one where all are welcome, regardless of ethnicity, gender, sexual identity, race, or age. The challenges faced by our students are daunting; the demographics are disturbing.

100% live below poverty level.

100% live in households dependent upon food stamps.

90% live in single parent homes.

100% qualify for free breakfasts and lunches.

84% of the student body is comprised of black teens who identify as male.

Only 15% have parents who are gainfully employed.

90% have at least one relative previously or currently incarcerated.

Maranathan Academy makes it possible for youth and adults trapped within the CAW to find success in the face of struggles, whether expected, such as lack of adequate food and clothing, or unimaginable, like a mother threatening her child's life for wanting to go to school.

Jewel

Tears filled Jewel's deep brown eyes during her senior review, a three-person conference designed to ensure students are on track with their goals. She was a timid twenty-seven-year-old honors student in Maranathan's Adult Studies program.

At the beginning of enrollment, each adult student is asked, "What caused you to drop out of high school?"

Jewel had been unable to answer then—the memories were too painful. A few weeks before graduation, she expressed a desire to motivate other adults needing a high school diploma and said she felt strong enough to share the challenges she'd experienced. In a voice filled with pain, Jewel revealed what, or rather who, had kept her from getting a diploma when she was a teen—her mother.

"Mama claimed she was scared that if I kept going to school, I'd be fast with boys. She started making me miss school when I turned sixteen, but I would still sneak out and go when she went to work."

"Why didn't she believe you just wanted to learn?" I asked.

"I don't know. I loved my mama, and I wanted to obey her, but I really wanted to get my diploma. When I got to be a senior, at the very beginning of the year, she told me I had to stop going to school. I snuck out and went anyway. One morning, she caught me and told me if I tried to go out the door and get on the bus, she would beat me to death." Jewel paused to compose herself, then continued. "I tried anyway, and she beat me so bad."

"Didn't you have any family who could help?" I asked.

"My grandaddy tried. I ran away to live with him, and he tried to enroll me in the school by his house, but my mama wouldn't give him any of my papers, and they couldn't enroll me without them. So, I gave up, started drinking, doing things with boys, got raped, ended up living in my car to get away from one boy I was living with. He was beating me."

The review moved on to the "satisfaction of academic requirements" and "post-graduation" sections. Jewel had already been accepted to the college of her choice but hadn't decided on a major.

"Any progress on picking a major?"

"Yes! Social work! I'm going to be a social worker."

"That's awesome! I cannot think of anyone who'd be a better one than you."

On her graduation day, Jewel smiled proudly as "Pomp and Circumstance" began to play, signaling the beginning of the ceremony. She wore the customary graduation regalia, complete with honor cord, and seemed to be walking on air as she received her diploma.

Her mother had refused to attend, but that was okay. Jewel's grandparents were there—cheering loud enough for ten people as they celebrated a gem of a young woman making her educational dreams come true.

Lethal Intellect

Although most of Maranathan's students have been expelled from public school systems for weapon-related or violent offenses, a small percentage of our student body is comprised of trauma victims—survivors of rape, molestation, and severe bullying. Many have attempted suicide—some repeatedly.

One of our current students vividly recalls the trauma he experienced in public school, which included verbal abuse, taunts over social media, and severe bullying that included physical assaults, all because he was a good student. In the CAW, it's dangerous to be smart.

Sam

"They saw my smartness as being weak, but I'm not weak!" said Sam. A bespeckled, fifteen-year-old gentle giant, he was already six feet tall and nearly two hundred pounds. "My mom told me not to fight people, so I tried not to, but I got picked on. This one dude kept picking on me. Said I was 'acting White.'"

Acting White is an unfortunate, urban stereotypical label given to students who make good grades and use traditional grammar when speaking.

Sam continued, "He jumped me. Then, two weeks later, he jumped me again. I fought back that time, and they suspended me."

"Did the school administrators know he'd been picking on you?" I asked.

"Yes, ma'am, but they said I should have just kept telling on him, not fight him back. They said I knew better."

Sam has found refuge at Maranathan Academy. Our zero-tolerance bullying policy makes it safe for kids to be smart. He is thriving academically and socially. With two part-time jobs, he's flourishing economically as well. Sam is trying to decide between attending college or expanding his uncle's landscaping business, one of his part-time jobs.

He has an awe-inspiring spirit of perseverance and shares a wonderful character trait with his fellow CAW intellectual refugees. Rather than settling for the status quo, he embraces every opportunity, buoyed by the discovery that success beyond any in his family's history is possible with willpower and hard work.

Chapter Four

Working in the Critically At-Risk World

Two big obstacles are frequently faced at Maranathan Academy. The first is the stigma that exists in the Black community, as well as others, relative to acknowledging and seeking treatment for issues involving anger management, substance abuse, and mental health. The second is ignoring obvious cries for help. Both obstacles often lead to serious consequences. Students blow educational opportunities or answer the call of the streets—becoming predators such as drug dealers and thieves or prey such as drug addicts and crime victims.

No matter which negative consequence befalls the student, the results are the same:

- Failure to reach full academic and occupational potential
- Inability to escape the CAW
- Becoming crime or poverty statistics instead of success stories

Although aware of the obstacles, a full understanding of the damage they cause didn't come until I founded Maranathan Academy and came face to face with stigma-induced loss and wasted opportunities.

Anger Management

Reggie

Though just twelve years old, Reggie stood over six feet tall and was the pampered only child of a single mother from an affluent Black family. He was in the seventh grade and had been expelled from a prestigious private school for fighting. It was his third expulsion. Reggie's mom, Ms. Marshall, blamed his previous schools for every bad thing that had befallen her son.

"They just blew things out of proportion. Never understood Reggie! He always said he was sorry, and they still put him out!"

Maranathan Academy was his last chance, and he did not fall within our usual demographics. His mother had a successful, highly lucrative career. She and Reggie lived in a prestigious residential golf community, moved about in wealthy circles, wore only designer clothes, and were decidedly elitist in their attitudes and conversations.

"I'm not sure how this is going to work out," Ms. Marshall said. "Reggie's never been around these kinds of people or gone to school in this kind of neighborhood. We'll see what happens."

"I'm not following you," I said, pretending not to understand her remarks.

"Well, you know, the housing projects and people from the housing projects, that's all."

"I know wonderful people who live in housing projects and awful people who live in mansions. It's the person, not the neighborhood, that counts. Good manners and behavior are required here, and I have no doubt that our students will treat Reggie well."

"Like I said, we'll see how it works out."

"If you're this uncomfortable, Ms. Marshall, perhaps you should try another school."

"There is no other school! I've heard how good you are with kids who get in trouble. We don't have a choice."

As the weeks passed, we learned Reggie wanted to be a rapper and resented his privileged life. He desperately wanted to be viewed as a thug, craved street cred, grew hostile when he couldn't have his way, and sulked—a lot.

While our students took pride in leaving the street life, Reggie bragged about the drug deals he planned to set up and asked our male-identifying students to join him. He was far from the misunderstood victim his mother had depicted. It was sad to see someone with every advantage in life pretending to be something he wasn't.

Our high school boys found him extremely annoying and refused to listen to him.

"Man, shut up! You don't know nothing 'bout weed or bricks! You need to sit down somewhere!"

The more they refused, the angrier Reggie became.

Theodore, whom we called "Tee," received the brunt of Reggie's anger.

Also, a seventh grader, Tee's life was an interesting mixture of contrasts. His mother was a hard-working nurse who had been raised in poverty along with her five brothers. She'd chosen to study and work her way out, was a model citizen, and steered clear of trouble. Her brothers had chosen the streets, rising quickly until they established positions of power. They had serious street cred and were Tee's heroes.

Tee's father had been raised upper middle class, found success in the corporate world, and was far from likable. After marrying Tee's mom and introducing her to an affluent lifestyle, he divorced her for a younger woman—leaving a then-eight-year-old Tee to be raised almost single-handedly by his heartbroken mom. Subsequently, Tee had a serious dislike for all things bougie, slang for rich or well-todo. Ironically, Tee's dad lived in the same exclusive community as Reggie and his mom.

Due to the street cred of his uncles and Tee's winning personality, our older boys loved him and treated him like a little brother. Reggie envied their mutual respect and affection.

Everything came to a head one day during final period. Reggie cracked on Tee. Cracking is an exchange of cutting jibes, a popular pastime that dates back at least a century and was once called "playing the dozens." It is a common and popular practice in urban neighborhoods where street sense and quick wit are mandatory. Due to its propensity to start fights, cracking is forbidden at Maranathan.

Tee had grown up surrounded by his uncles and their friends, all of whom were gifted in cracking. Reggie had only exchanged barbs with affluent young suburbanites like himself. In a battle of street witticism, he never had a chance.

Tee quickly opened his mouth to deflect Reggie's insult.

My "Stop it!" collided with Tee's retort, but it was too late.

Tee's rebuttal crack was so insultingly funny that I had to bite the insides of my cheeks and pinch myself to keep from laughing aloud.

The other students present made no such attempts. One boy laughed so hard that he actually fell on the floor and rolled.

Infuriated, Reggie jumped to his feet and charged Tee like an angry bull.

Ready for him, Tee stood and waited.

"Sit down! Stop!" I shouted, stepping in front of Tee and holding my hand out.

Still charging, Reggie ran smack into my hand.

"Who you pushing?" he demanded as he pulled back his arm and backhanded me across the left side of my face—hard.

My face exploded in pain, and I flew toward the fireplace, catching hold of the mantel just in time to avoid falling into the gas heater on the hearth.

The students' laughter stopped abruptly, replaced with deadly silence. They jumped up in unison to attack Reggie, who immediately ran and crouched behind me.

"Don't touch him! Sit down!" I ordered as the students remained standing and begged to retaliate on my behalf.

"Miss Dukes, let us get him! Please let us get him!"

"Reggie, go to the office. The rest of you, sit down, be quiet, and study. Do not leave this room."

When I entered the office, the apologies began.

"Miss Dukes, I'm so sorry! I didn't mean to hit you."

"Yes, you did."

"I was just so mad. I thought you were pushing me."

"No, you didn't. You were mad because I wouldn't let you hit Tee."

"Yes, ma'am, I was, but I'm sorry," he said, smiling and getting up from the chair in front of my desk.

"I accept your apology. Now sit down while I call your mother."

"You putting me out?" he yelled

"I'm suspending you."

"But I said I was sorry!"

"I believe you. You're still suspended."

Reggie glowered and began to lean forward toward the desk.

Feeling the need for additional distance, I added. "Go sit in the chair by the door."

He hesitated, then complied and gave me a pleading look.

"Can I still go on the field trip tomorrow?" "No."

"Please?" he said, adding a megawatt smile.

"No."

The smile vanished.

"This isn't fair! You're wrong! I said I was sorry!"

Knowing that Reggie's upbringing caused him to believe apologizing should make him immune to punishment, I prayed for calmness and remained silent, with the left side of my face throbbing painfully and my eye rapidly swelling shut.

Reggie's mother, Mrs. Marshall, didn't want him punished. She claimed I was "overreacting to getting hit" and tried to intimidate me into rescinding his suspension. First, with phone calls.

"Any other teacher would have just given Reggie a day in detention!"

"No, Mrs. Marshall, any other teacher would probably have called the police and had him locked up."

Next, she sent her uncle to take photographs of the students and staff as they entered the building. The police made him stop.

Last but not least, she called the city councilperson for Maranathan's district and lodged a formal complaint—which the councilperson refused to entertain.

The Academy's independent disciplinary committee called a conference. The suspension was upheld, and Reggie was recommended to attend school-sponsored counseling and anger management classes. His mom rejected the committee's decision and recommendation, choosing to rant instead. "You're putting Reggie out for no reason!" She then stormed out, yelling, "My child is not crazy!"

It was a disappointing outcome.

There was good reason to believe Reggie would have gained some benefit from anger management and counseling. Sadly, I think the stigma against receiving mental health services caused Ms. Marshall to reject the committee's recommendation and, in the process, deprive her son of the chance to be helped.

Substance Abuse

Greg

"So, you're seventeen years old and still in the seventh grade?" I asked the droopy-eyed teenage boy, who sat slumped in a disinterested posture with his legs sprawled out in front of him—ignoring my question. Being seventeen years old and still in the seventh grade wasn't Greg's only issue. He was also a gang member, a drug dealer, and, from the look of his glassy eyes, a customer as well. Crowded along with Greg in the small room that served as my office was his mother. Also in the room was my mother, Jacquelyn Bates Dukes, who, with a master's degree in guidance and counseling, often helped conduct interviews.

At Greg's lack of response, I rephrased the question.

"Still in middle school, Greg—why?" I asked with a hint of steel in my voice so he'd know not answering wasn't an option.

"'Cause. You know what I'm saying? That work they be giving us be too easy! So, when the teachers give it to me—I won't do it."

What? Is he serious?

Out loud, I said, "Let me get this straight. You could do the assignments, but to protest them being too easy, you just don't do them?"

"Yeahhhh," he drawled out as though he'd done something praiseworthy.

Mom had had enough. "Boy, that is not the way to hold a protest! Don't you see you're only hurting yourself? What do your teachers say while you keep failing?"

"They don't say nothing."

"Exactly!" Mom said emphatically. "Because you're not proving anything! Not doing the work makes them think you can't do it, not that it's so easy you won't do it."

We enrolled Greg and found him a quick study in every subject except math. Contrary to his assertions that the work at his previous school was "too easy," Greg found math hard. He was far below grade level. It wasn't that he couldn't learn. Somehow, he had not received proper instruction in the fundamentals that form the foundation for higher math. Subsequently, Greg struggled and refused to try and learn, which frustrated his math teacher—my mom. She could see that Greg actually had a gift for math, particularly measurements. His gift was evidenced by the fact that, though technically still in middle school, he successfully worked construction with his dad and his uncle—taking measurements, creating estimates for home repairs, laying tile, helping with welding jobs, and so on. Mom did everything she could to motivate Greg to complete his math assignments, all to no avail.

She begged.
He smirked.
She pleaded.
He laughed.
She tried incentives of his favorite candy and cookies.
He laid his head down on his desk and feigned sleep.

Finally, one day, amid a more exasperating than usual attempt to teach Greg math, my brilliant, strong mother did something she rarely did—she cried.

I don't think I've ever seen anything like the reaction her tears elicited. Greg's whole posture changed. He stopped slumping over, sat up straight, and said, "I'm sorry, Mrs. Dukes! I'm sorry!"

It was unquestionably his turning point. The rebellious, "I'm-not-even-thinking-about-what-you're-saying" smirk disappeared, and a genuine smile emerged—one that brought a sparkle to his eyes. From that day on, Greg became a model student in every subject.

He also allowed us to get to know the little boy hiding inside the body of a teenager pretending to be an adult. One day, Mom and I let him try some root beer that had become our favorite lunch staple. It was from a local health food store, and Greg loved it. We were glad but had no idea the root beer would be therapeutic. During one of our weekly group "rap" sessions, Greg shared that the root beer had replaced the malt liquor he'd once talked about with such fondness.

I'm always amazed by the big impacts little things can make on a critically at-risk student.

Years later, while being interviewed about Maranathan Academy helping to break cycles of juvenile offender recidivism, Greg mentioned Mom and revealed what had made him stop resisting her efforts to teach him—her tears.

He said, "I thought, wow, this lady is actually crying over me! Nobody had ever cried over me before. I couldn't believe she cared about me that much, and I thought, if this lady wants me to learn so bad she's crying, then I'm gonna try to learn." And he did.

After graduating with honors, Greg entered trade school and became a certified welder—marrying his longtime sweetheart along the way. He was hired by an independent welding shop owned by a wonderful man named Tom, who became his mentor. Greg never left Tom's side, and years later, upon retirement, Tom sold Greg the business.

So, this kid went from being a seventeen-year-old seventh-grade drug dealing substance abuser to being a devoted husband and father, proud homeowner, and small business owner. Greg is the epitome of what Maranathan Academy wants every critically at-risk student to become—a productive, contributing member of society.

Chapter Five

The Grey Zone

Working successfully in the CAW requires a willingness to recognize the existence of shades of grey and operate within what I call the grey zone. It houses a myriad of complex situations—such as a child being forced to choose between pursuing a fulfilling career or keeping a mother's love.

Jade

"My girlfriend needs to come to this school," said Paul, a senior at Maranathan.

He was a gregarious young man with delusions of grandeur and a beautiful, kindhearted mother, Ms. Michaels, who doted on and enabled him.

"Bring her to see me, and we'll see what we can do to help."

"Thank you, Miss Dukes. She's real smart! She's just going through some things right now with people doing her wrong."

Two days later, Paul and his mother walked into my office with one of the prettiest young ladies ever to cross Maranathan's threshold.

He introduced her as Jade. She was soft-spoken, extremely shy, and very respectful. While interviewing her, it became obvious that her shyness was the reason she had become the prey of people, instead of the predator her killer looks could easily have made possible.

I asked Jade if there were any colleges or careers she'd like to pursue after high school. She said she didn't know what college to attend or what she wanted to be, but she knew she wanted to "be somebody" and "do something" with her life.

I enrolled her immediately.

Jade was a great student who focused intently on her assignments and often reprimanded Paul for not focusing enough on his—thereby serving as a long-needed remedy to curb his mischief. We loved her!

One day, she came into my office and said, "Miss Dukes, can I talk to you about something?"

"Sure, sweetie. What's wrong?"

"My mama wants me to start dancing in a club."

"Why?"

"Cause I'm going to be eighteen next week, and we've been planning for me to do it for the longest."

Jade's upcoming eighteenth birthday was no surprise. We'd already included her name on our monthly birthday cake for students. However, hearing that her birthday would mark the start of a dancing career was a surprise—a big one.

"What kind of club is it, and do you want to dance there?"

"It's a strip club, and I did, but I don't, now."

My surprise now had a companion, joy, over the impact of Maranathan's mandatory career exploration classes. Jade had recently completed one. She'd shared with her instructor and classmates that caring for sick people had brought her joy from the time she was a little girl. The instructor directed her to a book on careers in nursing, and Jade made a wonderful discovery. She wanted to be a pediatric nurse.

"Have you told your mother you don't want to dance anymore"?

"Not yet. I'm scared."

"Do you want me to have her come in for a conference so you can tell her here instead of at home?"

"No, ma'am. I'll tell her by myself."

"Okay, but please let me know if I can help."

"Yes, ma'am. Thank you."

The news did not go over well.

"Jade saying she ain't gonna dance, and ain't gonna strip! She got to!" shouted Ms. Vaughn, Jade's mother, as she stormed into my office the next day—without an appointment and looking like she was out for blood.

"No, ma'am. She doesn't have to dance." I said soothingly. "She's found something she'd like to do more, something that will last a lot longer than "dancing" or stripping. Jade—"

"You don't know what you're talking 'bout!" Ms. Vaughn interrupted. "She gonna dance and strip and anything else she wants to do over there! Ain't nothing wrong with it! You seen that body! What else she gonna do with it?"

"Ms. Vaughn, you're absolutely right. There's nothing wrong with stripping if that's what a person wants to do. But Jade has a love for nursing. So, she's not going to strip. She's going to be a pediatric nurse."

Ms. Vaughn glared at me but took a seat.

Encouraged, I went on to explain that we would help Jade through the college admission process and that the guidance counselor would need copies of Ms. Vaughn's taxes so that we could help Jade complete the financial aid process, too.

Ms. Vaughn's eyes had narrowed to slits during my explanation.

And as soon as I stopped talking, the thunder fell.

Jumping out of her chair, she screamed, "You crazy as*h***! Jade gonna strip and make that money! That's what she gonna do!"

My hope that Ms. Vaughn's seated silence signaled her acceptance of Jade's new career choice fell by the wayside and was replaced with a painful realization. In her mind, Ms. Vaughn had already started spending the money Jade would bring into the household from stripping. There was no faulting the estimation of Jade's potential earning power as a stripper. With her looks and figure, she'd bring in a veritable windfall. What could be faulted was Ms. Vaughn's ability to assess career longevity—how long Jade would be able to dance.

I always tell my girls at Maranathan, "Study hard, ladies. Don't rely on your looks! Gravity is real!"

Doubting that she would appreciate me sharing that advice, I stayed silent while, still cursing, Ms. Vaughn gave me a death glare and left.

Concerned about what Jade might face when she got home, I began to pray.

A few hours later, I got a call. Ms. Vaughn had put Jade out of the house.

Livid, I immediately started trying to find her somewhere to stay. Here's where we enter the "grey zone." The only place that could provide Jade with some adult supervision and not leave her vulnerable to predators was her boyfriend Paul's house. While hardly an ideal living arrangement, I had to be realistic and look at the most prominent factors involved. There were three.

First, Ms. Vaughn had allowed Jade to spend the night with Paul for months. Second, Paul's mother knew Jade, loved her positive influence on her son, and said she'd happily take her in. Third, Jade living with her boyfriend and his mother was better than being forced to strip or live on the street.

Jade moved in, and the rest of her senior year went smoothly. Problem solved. After graduating from Maranathan with honors, Jade entered nursing school. Sadly, she and Paul went their separate ways. His thirst for fast money pulled him into a world she'd declined to enter even at the cost of parental disownment—a world of night clubs, strip clubs, stolen cars and drugs.

He opened several businesses that looked legit on the surface, making him appear a successful young businessman. But in reality, he was deeply engaged in the drug trade. Three years later, Paul was found shot to death just a few blocks from his house. No arrests were made, but speculation ran rampant in the streets about the reason for the hit, "He probably messed up somebody's money."

Rumors circulated that he was trying to take over a big dealer's territory. Regardless of the reason, the bottom line was that Paul, always ready with a scheme and a smile, was dead. It was yet

The Grey Zone

another senseless loss of a young life, one that pushed me to add a new program component and try to prevent another such loss among our students and alums.

Belief in the lyrics of some rap songs that make drug dealing seem glamorous causes many of the boys first entering Maranathan to think they're tough enough for "the game."

Fortunately, I have friends who have done serious time in penitentiaries for running major weight—dealing drugs—but were blessed to get out and turn their lives around. Paul's death prompted me to start a "From the Streets" speaker series and invite my friends to be presenters. Each quarter, students with signed parental or custodial permission slips hear my friends, the former weight-runners, share their stories in graphic detail. Hearing their stories confirms what we constantly tell the kids who aspire to deal drugs. "None of you have the stomach to do what it takes to rise to the top of that food chain." So far, we have a 92 percent success rate where wannabe drug dealers pick more honorable career choices.

As for Jade, even though they'd broken up, she deeply mourned Paul's death. Thankfully, she was strong enough to continue with her life and finish nursing school. She then married a great guy and enjoys a fulfilling career and a happy life.

Chapter Six

A Sneaky Form of Slavery: Government Assistance Dependency

There's never a dull moment at Maranathan Academy. Each day of the academic year is filled with intense situations ranging from tragedies borne from unfulfilled potential to triumphs attained via transformed lives. Both are fueled by the same source—dependency on government assistance. How it enslaves recipients, robbing them of ambition and hope, is heartbreaking. Watching individuals escape it is thrilling, and working to defeat it is an endless source of motivation.

The primary goal of Maranathan Academy is to break the intergenerational, cyclical dependency on government assistance that plagues the critically at-risk populace. To be clear, I am not referring to the government assistance received by individuals with mental or physical disabilities, senior citizens, or veterans. I am solely referring to the government assistance—more commonly known as welfare—provided to able-bodied individuals without requiring them to work.

Like government housing, government assistance is supposed to be a temporary fix, a way to get a leg up and attain the American dream. Unfortunately, it often misses the mark. Many who work in the CAW would agree that the amount of assistance received is meager and comes with strings attached that entrap instead of empower. The current system has loopholes that some recipients utilize to stay on welfare for decades. The result? Large groups of people develop a sense of entitlement, expect to be taken care of, and show great reluctance to or actually refuse to take advantage of opportunities for educational advancement or workforce training. Many from this group believe they have mastered "the game" and delight in their ability to collect assistance from multiple agencies—totally unaware that the sum total of all the assistance isn't enough for even a bare-bones quality of life.

My parents raised me to believe welfare was one of the worst things that ever happened to Black people. It's hard to argue against that viewpoint.

Look at the harm it does.

The spouse-induced reduction or termination of assistance discourages or prevents marriage. At the same time, the stipend increase for additional children incentivizes some women to view having babies as a cottage industry—and subsequently enlarge their families just so their checks can get bigger.

I walk through housing communities regularly and encounter female-led multi-generational assistance victims. Grandmothers, mothers, and daughters in the same family all living in the same housing community. Many grant me the privilege of their trust, and we have beautifully intense conversations. They share feelings of frustration and helplessness over economic struggles and living conditions. And they confide having realized too late that their stipends aren't enough to meet even the most basic needs of their children or themselves.

When I broach the subject of joining Maranathan's adult diploma completion program and share that college, career guidance, and personal care classes come with it, most refuse to consider enrolling. Some laugh at the idea that they could ever "get that piece of paper" or "be looking like I'm sophisticated." Instead, most express a resigned acceptance of lack. "I'm always gonna be struggling. That's just life."

Their words cause me pain. It's awful to hear women with so much potential be completely unaware of how beautiful and brilliant they are—or that escape from the whirlwind is possible. When I look into their despair-filled gazes, I am even more convinced that my parent's assessment of the destructive effect of welfare on the Black race was spot on.

Chapter Seven

Unintended Consequences

I treasure all chances to speak about the plight of the critically at-risk populace and explain my belief that the current government assistance system, revamped in 1996, needs revamping—again.

For example, some well-meaning person(s) in the government decided it would be a good idea to, via the SSI program, give a monthly stipend directly to parents whose children have been determined to be learning disabled. Should the child's school performance improve enough to remove the determination, the stipend, which many parents or guardians call a "slow learner check," is cut off. I assume the government person(s) thought the money would be used for tutorial services or to purchase educational materials. Unfortunately, in many cases, the check is used to purchase other things—which isn't surprising.

Critically at-risk parents live in poverty and experience tremendous economic struggle. Over time, I've observed that, after being constantly faced with needs and wants that exceed what their regular monthly stipends can purchase, many parents develop rationalization or entitlement mindsets, which create the perfect environment to mishandle the stipend and academically damage the children under their care. I and several fellow CAW workers have witnessed parents coaching their children to "act slow" in order to start or continue the receipt of a slow learner check.

The children are also discouraged from studying or learning to prevent the check from getting cut off.

It's tragic, yet not unexpected. Extreme lack or an entitlement mindset produces harmful results, such as CAW parents or guardians viewing an educational stipend as a "bonus" and feeling justified in using it to purchase other things. The purchases usually fall into two categories:

1. Essential items that food stamps aren't allowed to purchase, such as laundry detergent, soap, toilet paper, deodorant, et cetera. *Note: I find it ludicrous that assistance recipients aren't allowed to use food stamps for items needed for cleanliness and dignity.
2. Aspirational items, such as designer clothes or hair and nail salon visits—for the parent, not the child or children.

Entitlement mindsets must be counteracted. Maranathan Academy tries to dim the attractiveness of slow learner checks by providing wrap-around services, such as pantries for food and beauty, hygiene, and cleaning products. We also offer utility bill assistance and academic achievement gift cards. Additionally, we share graduate success stories and bring graduates back to speak.

These services help our parents and students facing extreme lack to look away from the stipend's shopping power and focus on the kind of success a good education makes possible.

Sadly, the wrap-around services rarely correct entitlement mindsets or convince parents to do without the aspirational purchases the stipend makes possible. Therefore, we who labor at Maranathan are forced to stand by helplessly as children—who are experiencing the joy of learning and becoming aware of the opportunities an education brings—are withdrawn. Maranathan Academy has an awesome graduation rate of 85 percent, but my heart breaks for the 15 percent we lose. Only 3 percent are lost due to bad behavior. The remaining 12 percent are withdrawn to ensure the continued receipt of a slow learner check.

Many parents and guardians in the CAW are willing to sacrifice chances for their children to be educated—sometimes with tragic results.

Jimmy

Naturally soft-spoken, Jimmy had been taught by his mother to pretend to be academically slow. He walked with his head down, his shoulders slumped, and mumbled monosyllabic replies to anything he was asked. An easy target for bullies, Jimmy had gotten into trouble for fighting to keep his sneakers from being taken. After enrolling in Maranathan and receiving individualized tutoring and plenty of encouragement from his teachers, something wonderful happened. Jimmy started learning.

He began to speak up, initiate conversations, and carry himself with new-found confidence. Next, he started to dream about the future and excitedly shared that he wanted to become a barber.

Maranathan Academy has an eleven-month school year that is divided into four quadmesters. Things were going great for Jimmy until end of quadmester grades were handed out during a quarterly conference, and his mother saw how well he was doing.

She came to withdraw him the next day.

As one of the few parents with a job, she'd been asked to pay a small tuition, had only done so once, and hadn't been hassled about it. Yet, on the day she came to withdraw him, Jimmy's mother said she couldn't afford the tuition.

I reminded her that we'd only inquired about his outstanding balance once and assured her Jimmy could continue attending Maranathan for free.

She offered another excuse for withdrawal. "I'm moving. He won't have a way to get here."

"We provide a monthly bus pass for students with transportation problems, remember?"

She acknowledged remembering, then finally just came out and said, "I'm pulling him out. I didn't know he was doing this good. You gonna get his check cut off!"

We continued to talk, and I learned that Jimmy hadn't been giving her the monthly progress reports we'd sent home. The quadmester report card had been his mother's first inkling of the academic ground he was gaining. She immediately went into what I call "check protection mode," where a parent or guardian withdraws a student to prevent them from learning. There was nothing I could do.

At only fifteen, Jimmy was too young to be placed in a part-time job and enrolled in our adult studies program. Nor could any help be given from an outside agency. After all, authorities can't intervene because a mother decides to put her child into a different school. Our hearts were broken.

The next month, I went to the high school commencement of a dear cousin. Over three days, Birmingham's public school system holds commencement exercises for each high school, using the same location but with staggered schedules. I was about to walk into the auditorium when I heard a voice hollering, "Miss Dukes!" I paused, turned around, and spotted a familiar face—Jimmy's.

"Jimmy! How are you, sweetie? I've been asking folks about you."

"Miss Dukes, I want to come back to the school."

"We never wanted you to leave! As soon as the graduation lets out, can I call your mom? Do you think she would let you come back?"

"Yes, ma'am. I've been asking her to, and she said she was going to let me come back."

Thrilled to hear Jimmy would be returning, I walked into the auditorium with a lighter step.

A short while later, while watching my cousin and her friends in their caps and gowns, I silently celebrated that Jimmy would soon be reunited with his school friends and would march to "Pomp and Circumstance" in the not-too-distant future. Only it didn't turn out that way. His mother neither answered nor returned my calls.

Unintended Consequences

Two weeks later, Jimmy was dead.

It turned out Jimmy's mother hadn't enrolled him in another school when she withdrew him from Maranathan. Never a streetwise boy, he had been going to a friend's house every day to play video games, trying to fill the hours while his mother was at work. Relatively innocent about the ways of the world, Jimmy hadn't realized his friend had a few gang members and lightweight drug dealers in his circle. One day, a rival gang drove by and shot up the house, missing everybody—except Jimmy. He died on the scene.

Had he been in school, Jimmy wouldn't have been shot. The tragic irony of his death hit me hard. He'd been withdrawn to ensure the continuance of a slow learner check. At the time of his withdrawal, several months remained before the SSI forms had been due on his school performance. By that time, Jimmy would have turned sixteen, been placed in a job with one of Maranathan's collaborative partners, and been able to contribute to his mother's household. Unable to see that, she'd withdrawn him and inadvertently caused his death—which had stopped the check immediately. She'd lost the money anyway.

That's why the cycle of dependency on government assistance must be broken—to prevent more senseless deaths of amazing children like Jimmy.

Chapter Eight

The CAW Journey

Working in the critically at-risk world is not for the faint of heart. Yet, a CAW career provides nearly indescribable joy and feelings of reward—the kind that only comes from walking in your purpose.

Me

Full disclosure: I wasn't going to be an educator. I was going to be an attorney and work exclusively with juvenile offenders. So, in my senior year of college, I volunteered at the local juvenile detention center and encountered something both shocking and heartbreaking. The kids in the facility were just that—kids, amazing kids who had done not-so-amazing things. Most had horrible home situations; many had learning disabilities, but all were eager to be taught. There was one problem. All the kids I met had been expelled from the Birmingham public school system. Some were as young as twelve years old, and several had expulsion terms of two years. After the expulsion period ended, they could re-enter their respective schools. However, they'd still be in the grades occupied at expulsion, leaving little incentive to return.

I tried to enroll them in different school systems and got another shock. In Alabama, when one public school system expels a student, none of the other school systems have to accept him/her/

them. Therefore, the student is expelled from every school system in the entire state! I began to feel that I should start a school for expelled students but quickly went into prayer mode to push that feeling aside. From as far back as elementary school, I'd planned to be a lawyer, and nothing was going stop me! I approached private schools to enroll the kids but quickly hit a brick wall. None were willing to accept expelled students. These kids had no options for enrollment, and the obstacles I encountered began to feel like divine intervention.

Still, I resisted starting a school and looked for non-traditional education options. I found only one to explore—home school. It was a dead end. Lack of education or interest, coupled with economic hardships for the kids' parents and guardians, made home-schooling impossible. Cue the return of the feeling that I should start a school for kids no one else would work with—expelled kids being denied a second chance. This time, there was no praying it away. The feeling had brought some company. Memories of the lessons taught and examples set by my school teacher mother and vocational rehabilitation counselor father came flooding in, such as the many times mom welcomed students into our family and purchased necessities for them so that they could have a support system, the times she'd cried after circumstances beyond their control played a part in their being expelled or forced to drop out of school. The way my father had literally laid his life on the line during the Birmingham Civil Rights Movement—I'll offer more details about his selfless bravery later—or the way he would go above and beyond the call of duty to make sure clients could re-enter society after serving time in prison or successfully completing drug rehab. Time and time again, my mom's former students or my dad's former clients would come up to us in a grocery store or restaurant and thank them for having helped when no one else would.

Service, speaking truth to power, and helping people was in my DNA. For me, to see a wrong being done and ignore it or look the other way when someone was in need of help wasn't possible. So, I gave in to the feeling. If a white flag had been handy, I would have waved it. As far as I was concerned, the Lord had changed the direction of my life.

There was only one thing left to do—tell my parents.

"Guys, I'm not going to law school. I'm going to start a school for the kids no other schools will work with."

My mother's support was immediate. She was a teacher whose classes were always filled with the students her fellow teachers couldn't handle.

"Yes!" she yelled, pumping her fist in the air, obviously thrilled by my announcement.

My father, Reverend Frank Dukes, had a different reaction. "Nooo! You're valedictorian! You're summa cum laude! You can't do this to me!"

He was a counselor for the Alabama State Department of Education's Vocational Rehabilitation division. With a caseload solely focused on alcoholics, drug addicts, and public offenders, he did not want his daughter to embark on a career in the social service arena.

I don't call my dad "Dad." I actually call him "Son," not in a flippant way, but as a term of affection that began years ago.

One day, as was his custom, he went to kiss Mom and me goodbye before he left the house. For some reason, when he bent, kissed me on the cheek, and said, "Bye, Daughter."

I replied, "Bye, Son."

He straightened, started toward the door, then stopped midstride, turned around with a smile, and said, "Did you just call me, 'Son?'"

I said, "Yes, sir."

"Okay, bye, Daughter," he said, and he's been Son ever since.

Some people think it's strange, but it works for us.

Back to his reaction. Son listed all the reasons why I shouldn't abandon my plans for law school, shared how much he had looked forward to bragging about his daughter being in law school, and then waited expectantly for my reply.

"Son, I'm sorry. I have to do this."

I guess he saw the determination in my eyes because he fell silent, then nodded his acceptance.

May of 1991 marked my graduation from Miles College. Mom announced her retirement so she could help me with the school, and on September 3, 1991, Maranathan Academy began with one student, one table, and four chairs. Funding was tight—in other words, nonexistent. Living at home rent-free and Mom generously giving me an "allowance" made it possible for me to stay the course. By the way, Son became one of Maranathan's biggest supporters and even served as an adjunct faculty member after he retired.

In 1999, Maranathan Academy was inducted into the archives of the Birmingham Civil Rights Institute for being the first school of its kind in the state of Alabama. It's still the only nonprofit private school in Birmingham that works exclusively with critically at-risk students. Maranathan Academy is also the only nonprofit, private school in Birmingham that will accept students expelled for weapons-related or violent offenses.

To date, Maranathan has graduated nearly 400 students, impacted the lives of more than 2,000 members of the critically at-risk populace, and now counts law school graduates, medical professionals, mechanics, bankers, welders, law enforcement officers, members of the United States armed forces, and more among its alumni.

I love working in the CAW and wake excited every day to get to the office. It's amazing what happens when you let go of your plan and allow yourself to be placed on a path that makes it possible for you to walk in your purpose.

Chapter Nine

Scenes from a Parallel Universe

In many ways, the critically at-risk world is a uniquely managed parallel universe in that its citizens reside within mainstream society but exhibit paradoxical behaviors for success. Trapped in the cycle of dependency on government assistance, many critically at-risk students and their families find themselves on one of three life paths: illegal activities, jobs that provide abundant work hours but neglect to pay livable wages, or the creation of schemes and scams.

Many of Maranathan's parent or guardian population appear to possess a unique way of thinking regarding getting a job or attaining a certain standard of living.

They want to enjoy the comforts of life, but they don't want to work.

One of my mom's pre-Maranathan Academy teaching experiences provides a prime example.

Daphne

In 1975, Marie was one of Mom's brightest students.

"Mrs. Dukes," Marie told her, "Daphne deposited that check you gave her!"

"What are you talking about?"

"One of those checks you gave us when you taught us how to write checks!"

"No, she couldn't deposit that check. It's not real."

"Yes, she did, Mrs. Dukes! Daphne and her mama took it to the bank and deposited it."

"She did, Mrs. Dukes! She did!" added Robert, another student.

Could it be possible?

Mom started thinking about how nice Daphne had been dressed the day before. Her usually unkempt hair had been freshly styled, and she was wearing what appeared to be a new outfit—a marked departure from her usual well-worn clothes and shoes. Mom had complimented her. "Daphne, baby, you look so pretty!"

A sweet little girl in a family with many kids and a mom and dad who could never make ends meet, Daphne had just smiled.

Marie's words made Mom remember something else—Daphne's sudden ability to buy ice cream during lunch the previous day.

Still, Mom couldn't believe that Daphne and her mom had been able to deposit a practice check from a math lesson.

Mom loved math! In fact, she had a double major in chemistry and mathematics. A firm believer that mastering the life skills unit of math textbooks was an essential part of education, Mom annually went to a local bank and got practice checks—to afford her students a realistic learning experience. Although the size of regular checks, they sported a fake address ending in "Anywhere, USA" and were obviously not real.

Surely, there's no way the bank let them deposit that check!

But it had! A quick talk with Daphne revealed that the kids were right. Mom went to the principal and called the bank, which promptly investigated. Sure enough, the check, written for $500.00, had been deposited, and all but $10.00 had been spent. The bank manager was mortified! The principal called Daphne's mother, Mrs. Campbell, and let her know he knew what had been done. Typical of someone with an entitlement mindset, she blamed Mom!

Mrs. Campbell came to the school the next day, interrupted Mom's class, and confronted her for "giving Daphne that bogus check."

Mom asked her to come with her to the principal's office. Once there, she and the principal took turns trying to get Mrs. Campbell to understand.

"You knew you didn't have any money in the bank. You knew that check was not real. No one did anything wrong to you. You were wrong."

"Naw, it's y'all! Y'all shouldn't be giving out bogus checks to children!"

She even went so far as to report Mom to the school system's superintendent.

Can you imagine what might happen if this situation occurred in education's present climate? An administrator or social media powered court of public opinion might suggest that practice checks should not be utilized as a teaching tool because some impoverished students might mistakenly think they're real.

Blessedly, the Daphne incident occurred when administrators usually respected and supported teachers. So, despite Mrs. Campbell's accusation that her daughter had been given a bogus check, the superintendent sided with Mom and her principal, and things returned to normal.

Before judging Daphne's mother or Jimmy's mother from Chapter Seven, understand that they're victims of a system that was created to help but inadvertently hurts.

Here's a standard argument used whenever individuals challenge my quest to help Maranathan's primarily Black student body escape cyclical dependency on government assistance: "There are more Whites on welfare than Blacks!"

I agree, then point out that, although there are more Whites on welfare than Blacks, people of color are disproportionately represented in receiving government assistance. As of the 2020 U.S. Census, Whites comprise 59.3 percent of the U.S. populace and 43 percent of the country's welfare recipients. Hispanics comprise 18.9 percent of the US populace and 28 percent of the country's welfare recipients. However, Blacks comprise 12.4 percent of the U.S. populace and 23 percent of U.S. welfare recipients. That's nearly double our actual percentage in the entire country's populace! For a racial group to be only 12.4 percent of a country's populace but account for nearly a quarter of persons receiving government assistance is troubling.

The disproportionate disparities don't stop there.

At 59.3 percent of the U.S. populace, Whites comprise 30.3 percent of the country's penitentiary inmates, with 89 percent of the inmates classified as male and 10.4 percent as female.

Hispanics account for 18.9 percent of the U.S. populace. Yet, Hispanics are 23.3 percent of U.S. penitentiary inmates, with 95 percent classified as male and 5 percent as female.

Although Blacks are only 12.4 percent of the U.S. populace, we account for 33 percent of penitentiary inmates. Of that 33 percent, 96 percent are classified as male, and 4 percent are classified as female.

Blacks who identify as male have the odds stacked against them as it pertains to the probability of being incarcerated. According to a powerful bullet point contained in the "Prisoners in 2020 Statistical Tables" report from the U.S. Department of Justice's Office of Justice Programs Bureau, "Black males were 5.7 times as likely to be imprisoned in 2020 as White males; black males ages 18 to 19 were 12.5 times as likely to be imprisoned as white males of the same age."

There are 1,021,288 sentenced prisoners under the jurisdiction of U. S. state correctional facilities. 332,000 are Black. 321,700 are White. 224,300 are Hispanic. 12,500 are Asian and 15,600 are Native American/Alaska Native. Of the total number of U.S. sentenced prisoners under the jurisdiction of state correctional authorities, 62.9% have been convicted of violent crimes. The violent crime category is comprised of: murder, negligent manslaughter, rape/sexual assault, robbery, aggravated/simple assault, and other.

As it pertains to race in this category, among the 332,000 Black sentenced prisoners, 68.4% have been convicted of violent crimes. Yet, in what I view as data capable of shattering a stereotype widely bandied about by White supremacists and fear mongers, only 9.8

percent of the 68.4% of Black sentenced prisoners convicted of violent crimes have been convicted for rape or sexual assault, as compared to 19.8 percent of Whites, 19.1 percent of Hispanics, 15.6 percent of Asians and 13.9 percent of Native Americans/Alaska Natives sentenced prisoners.

The crimes that account for most of the Black sentenced prisoners convicted of violent crimes are robbery at 18.6 percent and murder at 18.7 percent. These percentages are tragically explainable. A 2020 article by Gerard Torrats-Espinosa notes that "children living in disadvantaged neighborhoods are forced to develop strategies to navigate threatening public spaces and change their daily routines and patterns of social interaction." Torrats-Espinosa goes on to say, "Neighborhood violence undermines the quality of life in entire communities, transforms the sociodemographic composition of neighborhoods, and leads to public and private disinvestment (Morenoff and Sampson 1997; Sampson 2012; Skogan 1986)."

In my opinion, such forced sociological adaptability and disinvestment can result in persons accepting or participating in unacceptable behavior such as property or even violent crimes.

Torrats-Espinosa's findings are also supported by a 2021 research article regarding "youth violence" in a "low-income, urban community". The following were identified as "factors" by study participants: "(a) social and behavioral norms, (b) lack of resources, (c) systems that perpetuate concentrated disadvantage, (d) needs for prosocial development, (e) stress and trauma, (f) parenting challenges, (g) media, and (h) drugs and alcohol."

I'm convinced there is a direct correlation between the aforementioned data and study results and the disproportionate percentage of Blacks dependent on government assistance. Even more disparities could be mentioned. However, I'll refrain from doing so and simply make this statement: There is work to be done, and time is of the essence!

The longer residents of the CAW remain unaware that education can help them stop depending on the government for survival, the harder it becomes for them to embrace opportunities and become productive, contributing members of society.

Two requisites exist for ending cyclical dependency on government assistance:

1. Acknowledging that such dependency has unintentional, long-reaching consequences, such as the creation of generations of people mired in poverty and hopelessness.
2. Changing the way recipients of government assistance are viewed and treated.

Grace's mom is an example. Remember Grace, the twelve-year-old expectant mother featured in the Prologue whose mother, Katrina, was calculating how much extra money Grace's soon-to-be-born son would bring into the household? Rather than being repulsed or passing judgment, put yourself in her shoes. At the time of Grace's pregnancy, Katrina was only twenty-seven. She'd given birth to Grace at the age of fourteen. Her mother had given birth to her at thirteen and died from breast cancer before she was thirty, leaving Katrina at the mercy of relatives who saw her as nothing more than a check.

So, to Katrina, little girls getting pregnant was normal, and showing excitement over the additional check a new baby brings was traditional. In other words, she was just doing what had been done to her, viewing a baby as an extra source of income rather than a defenseless, precious human being who should be loved and protected. Katrina's not a monster. She's an ideological casualty.

Bring Katrina to mind whenever someone needs help in understanding that persons dependent on government assistance aren't bad people. They're victims suffering from broken spirits, brought on from being conditioned and programmed by the system to accept a life of struggle.

Tragically, the realization that they're victims often dawns too late, yet another mark against a flawed system that inadvertently enslaves the people it was created to help.

Chapter Ten

You May Now Enter the Whirlwind

It's easy to get trapped within the cycle of dependency on government assistance, but it's hard to escape. Consider the following simulation.

You're a seventeen-year-old girl raised by a single mother in a government housing community and have just found out you're pregnant. No one gets upset when you tell them. This isn't surprising because every woman in your immediate family had her first baby as a teenager.

You think things will be easy because your pregnancy comes with "help:"

- Prenatal care at the free clinic
- WIC—the government's Special Supplemental Nutrition Program for Women, Infants, and Children
- Food stamps
- Childcare assistance

All goes well. You deliver a healthy baby and have doctor's excuses for your pre-natal appointments and hospital stay. But your postpartum recovery period exceeds what your doctors deem "necessary," and you fail your classes due to excessive absences. Embarrassed to be in the same grade the next school year, you decide to drop out and get a job. While job hunting, you discover that not having a diploma limits you to job opportunities with terrible pay and no benefits and that getting a job will cut off or reduce your monthly assistance.

Next, you learn that you will be able to get your own housing community apartment when you turn nineteen, or before if you decide to become an emancipated minor.

Now, nineteen and out on your own, things are wonderful. For the first time in your life, you have your own room. You have met a nice guy with a part-time job, and he is attending trade school. He also wants to marry you and adopt the baby. You love him, but welfare benefits decrease when a family's income increases. Therefore, marrying your guy will end or seriously reduce your assistance, and your rent will increase if he moves in. If you marry and move into a house subsidized through Section 8, you'll probably lose the house after he graduates and gets a full-time job.

Unwilling to "struggle on just what he makes" or to get a job to create a two-income household and fight for a better life, you break up with him and meet a guy who:

- Doesn't work
- Is fine with staying in your apartment and hiding in a closet during housing authority inspections
- Enjoys living off your food stamps and government assistance stipend

Soon, you're pregnant with baby number two. Your food stamp allotment and monthly assistance stipend increase, but neither lasts until the end of the month.

Seeing your children go without compels you to begin studying for your GED. Your boyfriend says, "You don't need it!" and gets violent.

You're afraid but have no way to escape. Everyone you know lives in your housing community—including your mother, right next door.

You give up, stop attending GED class, and live trapped in a whirlwind of struggle, hopelessness, and despair.

It happens just like that. Whirlwind 1. Victim 0.

I'm not a policy maker, but situations frequently encountered on my CAW work journey give me the confidence to express the following opinions:

1. The current system of government assistance is broken, and a new revamp is urgently needed.
2. Courses on financial literacy should be mandatory for all recipients of government assistance and include a section on the true cost of raising a child from infancy to adulthood, which is the age of eighteen; exceptions and or modifications should be made for disabled recipients.
3. A one-time, eight-to-twelve-week parenting class should be mandatory for all assistance recipients. Parent support groups should be made available, and incentives should be given for participation.
4. Distribution of information to assistance recipients, regarding the importance of education or workforce training, as well as referrals to resources for each, should be a high-priority system component.
5. Proof of the pursuit of education or work, volunteer or paid, should be requisite for initiating and continuing assistance during the allotted five-year time limit.
6. The loopholes which allow assistance recipients to stay on longer than five years need to be tightened. For example:

    a. The federal sixty-month time limit for assistance does not apply to state-funded benefits, thereby opening the door for multiple enrollment extensions.

    b. A large number of welfare cases are categorized as "child-only." In other words, the children in the household receive the assistance, not the adults. However, the adults are in charge of making purchases with the funds. I have observed that the child-only categorization allows parents or guardians to live

off the stipends received by their children, thereby making it possible for them not to work.
7. Incentives need to be given to recipients trying to improve their circumstances by working or attending school.

Implementing any of these suggestions will, in my opinion, help immeasurably. However, I firmly believe education to be the most effective component in helping assistance recipients attain self-sufficiency. Maranathan's adult diploma completion program often serves as a catalyst for escaping the whirlwind of government assistance dependency—especially for single moms who want to create better lives for their families.

Imani

Imani was a bright young woman, but a pregnancy during the second semester of her senior year had caused her to drop out of high school. Years passed, and she found herself stuck in a dead-end job earning only $9.50 an hour. She could not provide even basic needs for herself, her six children, or her chronically ill mother, for whom she was the primary caregiver. She needed a chance and found one through Maranathan Academy's Adult Diploma Completion Program.

Imani graduated with honors and, armed with a high school diploma, became a licensed contractor who quickly gained success, purchasing her first home one year later. She now earns over $65,000 a year.

The privilege of helping an amazing person, such as Imani, escape cyclical dependency on government assistance fuels my determination for Maranathan to remain a fixture in the CAW.

PART 2
Cycle Breakers That Set the Stage for Success

Chapter Eleven

Getting the Backstory

Working successfully with critically at-risk students depends on getting what I call the backstory, circumstances that cause negative behavior. Many are overwhelmed by great pain, which causes them to suffer silently, behave badly, or put themselves in danger. The latter two are cleverly disguised cries for help and attention. Without the backstory, it's easy to categorize CAW students as "problem students" instead of youth or adults who need help.

Jason

Rage brought Jason and his mother to my office for an enrollment interview. She wore a clerical badge and a nervous smile. He sported close-cropped hair, brushed and trained until it lay in waves. He sat calmly, but his eyes were so filled with anger that they practically crackled each time he blinked, giving him the appearance of the stereotypical "angry Black youth."

His disciplinary record matched the anger in his eyes—multiple fights, verbally abusive altercations with teachers, and numerous suspensions. His last fight had been serious enough to result in him being expelled from public school. During the expulsion hearing, school administrators described Jason as "a little thug" who "was headed to jail" if he didn't "straighten out."

The hearing officer's report stated Jason "showed no remorse for his actions." I asked him about the incident from the report. As he spoke about the fight and the injuries he inflicted, the hostility and barely contained fury of his tone made him seem incapable of calmness, regret, or love. But I spotted a large tattoo on his arm that negated that assumption. The tat was just one word, the name Monique. When asked about Monique's importance to him, the tears that filled his eyes and the tat's prominent placement and beautiful design let me know that Jason was a kid in pain who felt things deeply.

He had been a model student until his tenth-grade year. One Saturday night, two police officers notified the family that Monique, Jason's oldest sister, had been murdered.

Three men had broken into her apartment, shot her, put her in the bathtub, and set her on fire. The family was devastated. Prior to Monique's murder, they had been a close-knit unit comprised of two parents, two daughters, and one son. Now, a vital part of that unit was gone. After the funeral, detectives working the case discovered that one of the three men who'd committed the murder was the boyfriend of Jason's other sister—a man Jason had looked up to as a big brother.

Can you imagine learning that, for all practical purposes, your brother helped murder your sister? Jason, only fifteen at the time of the murder and unable to process the tragedy, quickly drifted into a dark place. When he returned to school, grief and rage had turned him into a powder keg. So much so that any comment—even a casual, "Hey Jason, what's going on?"—earned the speaker a punch in the face.

We worked with Jason academically and spiritually and got him counseling, the latter of which was initially resisted by his parents.

"He doesn't need counseling. If he did, our pastor would have told us. He talked to Jason when he first started getting into trouble and said all he needed to do was get in that Bible—get him some strength."

Getting the Backstory

Being careful not to insult their faith, I pointed out that a family member's brutal murder is hard for adults to process, much less teenagers. I was concerned that if Jason didn't receive professional counseling, he might be lost, too. His parents relented, and in the following weeks, Jason slowly broke free of the grief-fueled rage that had almost consumed him. That newfound freedom allowed us to help him get a job, and he became one of the main sources of laughter at Maranathan by recounting stories from work.

Jason is a poster child for the importance of obtaining a student's backstory. Having it helped us help him succeed. He earned his high school diploma, became a much in demand auto mechanic, and is a model citizen. His big sister would be proud.

Chapter Twelve

Facilitating Chip Removal

In my experience, it is imperative that all "chips" be removed from the shoulders of our students—particularly chips that are anti-inclusive, anti-work, or racist. Removing chips helps critically at-risk students break free from mindsets that obstruct pathways to success. Therefore, we encourage cultural awareness and celebration while working tirelessly to help our students eradicate negative thoughts or perceptions of their own race or of the races, ethnicities, and identities of others.

Chip # 1: The Racism Chip

Laura

Critically at-risk students are often marginalized and treated with disdain or disgust. In many instances, they've been made to feel inferior, which makes them vulnerable to individuals who sow divisiveness, primarily along racial lines. As a result, many of our students express distrust or dislike for persons from middle to wealthy socioeconomic classes—specifically Whites or people of color (POC) from other countries.

Because of that mistrust, Maranathan makes a concerted effort to broaden the horizons and awareness of our student body by seeking the involvement of people from different ethnicities, faiths, and walks of life. Why? To show that being melanin blessed should not be a prerequisite for friendship, fellowship or trust. It's important for our students to understand that regardless of appearance, income bracket, race, ethnicity, gender, or sexual identity, to quote and paraphrase Ann Lamotte and Maya Angelou, respectively, ". . . we're . . . more alike than we are different."

Attorney Charlie Waldrep is a longtime supporter of Maranathan Academy. He came from very humble beginnings and has a great love for underserved communities. Charlie delivers a motivational talk each academic year and gives each student a generous gift card at Christmastime. In short, he's wonderful.

Unfortunately, the first time he gave out the gift cards, I didn't realize the parents of some of our students would take the cards or guilt the students into buying things for other family members. When I found out, I was livid and vowed it would not happen again. That vow birthed an annual field trip to take the kids shopping so they can spend the cards largely on themselves.

The day of our third annual Christmas shopping trip dawned crisp but sunny, and our kids were eager to get going. Since Maranathan doesn't have a van, we often use faculty vehicles and carpool for short excursions. As the daughter of a U.S. Army veteran, I understand the beauty and peacekeeping power of a carefully crafted deployment list.

At 9:00 a.m. sharp, with a few supplemental cars set to arrive momentarily, we went outside to load up. Laura Pitts, our yoga teacher, is a raven-haired, brown-eyed beauty. She's a volunteer instructor who spends a lot of time at Maranathan. In addition to yoga, she teaches breathing techniques to stave off or help manage feelings of anger and anxiety. The students adore her.

She also drives a Porsche.

Needless to say, everyone, including some of the faculty, wanted to ride with her. I began calling out the car assignments. "Stephanie, James, and Carl, you're in Mrs. Pitts's car." Carl hadn't been with us long and had a horrible time remembering names.

Facilitating Chip Removal

"Mrs. Pitts?" he asked.

Smiling, I said, "Your yoga teacher, Carl. Y'all help him remember who she is before she pulls up."

Descriptions began to fill the air, "The lady with the long hair. The lady who comes on Wednesdays."

Carl still couldn't place her.

Laura's imminent arrival and my desire for a speedy departure prompted me to say, "The White lady with long black hair."

Three sets of surprise widened eyes turned to me. Almost in unison, they said, "Mrs. Pitts is White?"

Comments began to ring out. "I just know she teaches us yoga. I don't think about her being White, for real."

I wanted to jump for joy! The teachings and interaction had worked. They didn't see Laura as a "White" woman. They just saw her as a lady who cared enough about them to teach them how to breathe and master the fundamentals of yoga. Her race wasn't a factor.

"Yes," I said. "Mrs. Pitts is White, and she's about to pull up."

Not two minutes later, Laura arrived. We departed, reached the mall a short time later, and reminded our students of their mandates. First, at least $35 must be spent on merchandise for their personal use. Second, shoplifting would result in the student or students involved being left with store security and suspended pending a hearing that would, 99.5 percent of the time, result in their being expelled.

With that, the shopping began, and I found myself smiling wider than usual, elated that we had knocked the racism chip off the shoulders of yet another group of kids.

Chip # 2: The Anti-Inclusion Chip

Mike

Maranathan holds weekly student rap sessions where our students can vent about what's happening in the world and in their lives.

One of our newer students opened up to the group about a recent trauma. His name was Sebastian, and he had enrolled a few months earlier after being severely beaten for being gay by some classmates in public school. His remarkable story is detailed in Chapter Seventeen.

Sebastian's trauma occurred over the weekend when he and two female friends had gone to the movies and encountered a group of guys from his old school. While they all stood in line, the boys taunted him for being gay.

Sebastian shared that the boys' taunts and aggressiveness had scared him and reminded him of a time he was beaten for being gay. Suddenly, Mike, a student expelled from public school for severely beating a gay teen, interrupted, angrily saying, "Man! They did you like that, man?"

Startled, Sebastian nodded his head and timidly replied, "Yes."

"Man, the next time somebody do you like that, you call me, man! I'll get my boys, and we'll come up there, man, and we'll—" He trailed off, looked at me, and said, "Miss Dukes?"

"Yes?" I said, arching an eyebrow and tilting my head.

"That's what I did, isn't it?"

"Yep, it sure is."

At that moment, without another word being spoken, Mike and I knew he'd never harm a gay person again. Being in school with Sebastian and getting to know him had shown Mike that every negative thing he had been taught to believe about gay people was wrong—the stereotypes, hatred-filled monologues delivered by family and friends—all wrong. Maranathan had allowed him to see Sebastian as he was—a human being, a kid just like him who deserved to live, laugh, and love in safety.

So, when people skeptically ask, "Juvenile offenders and trauma victims together in the same school, really, Donna?"

I just smile and say, "Yeah. We have the persecuted and persecutors learning side by side, and it works."

Chip #3: Anti-Employment and Anti-Early Parenthood Combo Chip

Jason Part Two

At Maranathan Academy, the importance of a strong work ethic is emphasized, and accepting personal responsibility for one's actions is mandatory. We strive to help our students develop a strong character steeped in compassion and empathy, embrace moral values and ethics, and understand their responsibilities to themselves, the community, and our country.

Nothing accomplishes that faster for a CAW resident than getting a job, which is why a part-time job is a requirement for Maranathan Academy students. Remember Jason from Chapter Eleven?

Like most of his classmates who identified as males, he didn't believe he would live to see twenty-one and wanted to leave a legacy. Also, like most of his classmates, he had devised a plan to ensure his ability to do so. A self-proclaimed pretty boy, Jason proudly shared that he planned to continue the family tradition of "finding a good woman and having some kids off the jump" (right away). Working or ensuring he could take care of the kids was neither a factor nor a consideration. Most of the men in his family didn't work. Therefore, he balked at the part-time job requirement. We explained the method of the requirement's "madness:"

- Working and staying out of the streets just might help him live past twenty-one
- A feeling of satisfaction comes from earning your own money
- Most importantly, we weren't going to budge

Jason gave in gracefully and was quickly hired by a grocery store. His outgoing personality and exceptional work made him a customer and company favorite. He racked up many hours and bragged to everyone at school about how fat his first check would be.
Bless his heart.

The morning after his first payday, Jason ran into my office, waving his check.

"Miss Dukes, look at my check!"

I did, then asked, "What's wrong?"

"What happened to all my money?! I'm supposed to have more than this!"

"They cut you for taxes."

"But why so much?"

I started pointing to each "cut" and explaining its usage. He was fine until I mentioned welfare and assisting women who had babies they couldn't afford.

"I didn't tell them to have those babies!"

"No, but you're helping to pay for them."

With quiet fury, he vowed to make up for the cuts by working more hours, then proceeded to show the check to his classmates, explain the cuts, and loudly proclaim he wasn't "having kids for a long time," and he didn't.

Best birth control ever!

Chapter Thirteen

Education and Encouragement

Marquita

"I need to be in a smaller classroom, somewhere with less people where the teachers get to teach, and they care about you. If I could do that, I could learn," explained Marquita, a seventeen-year-old who craved academic success.

"What are your grades like now?" I asked.

"Mostly Bs, Cs, and a few Ds, but I know I can do better! I know I can make good grades. It's just hard where I am."

"Have you been in any trouble, had any fights?"

"No, ma'am. I—"

"She hasn't been in any fights. She's not one of those girls always getting in trouble," Interrupted Mrs. Drake, Marquita's mother. "Quita is quiet, but she has to sit in there with all those other kids who be acting up and keeping the teacher from teaching!" she said disgustedly.

Marquita resumed speaking, "Sometimes the kids be playing cards in the classroom. They throw paper at the teacher, talk on their phones, fight. It's awful!"

"What do the teachers do when the kids act up?"

"Nothing," Marquita said. "They act like they're scared to say anything."

Having visited her school, I didn't doubt one word she was saying. I'd been invited to speak at a Black History assembly, along with a shero, which is how I refer to women I consider heroines. Knowing my students would benefit from the program, I decided to make it a field trip. Long story short, while on stage, I saw two male students in the audience engaged in a heated argument. Teachers lined the auditorium's walls, but not one of them intervened. It was obvious the argument could turn physical, and it did. All of us on stage watched helplessly as fists started flying. An assistant principal and a coach who had just entered the auditorium waded into the fray together and stopped the fight.

I was flabbergasted that none of the teachers tried to help, not even when their colleagues, the coach and assistant principal, intervened. Later that day, in an attempt to make sense of the inaction, I contacted a friend who had been in the auditorium and asked what was going on at the school. She gave me an earful, describing the school as a war zone, averaging six fights a day at minimum. Teachers who tried to intervene were often threatened by students and received no support from the administration, so they decided not to attempt to prevent or stop the fights.

Bringing my focus back to the present, I resumed the interview with Marquita. "What do you plan to do when you graduate?" I asked.

"I'm going to go to the Army."

I love for my students to enlist and serve our country. In Marquita's case, however, I had a gut feeling she was better suited for a different career.

After concluding the interview questions, I stood, shook hands with mother and daughter, and welcomed them to Maranathan.

Marquita's enrollment made two groups very happy. The boys were thrilled because she enlarged Maranathan's always small percentage of students who identify as female. The faculty was elated because few things bring teachers greater joy than working with students who want to learn.

Education and Encouragement

I shared our faculty's joy and celebrated a premonition. My gut told me Marquita was going to soar to heights she had no idea she could reach, and I was thrilled that I would have the privilege of taking part in her journey.

Having a school with caring administrators and teachers turned out to be the missing piece of the puzzle for Marquita. For the first time ever, she felt safe learning and show her smarts. She was an absolute delight to teach, and everyone rejoiced as Marquita became the social and academic all-star she was always meant to be. She was a constant fixture on the honor roll, queen of the senior prom, and— drumroll please—valedictorian of her graduating class.

Still unconvinced that the military would best fit her, I asked Marquita and her mom if they would consider college. Her mother was wary. Several of her friends had allowed their daughters to leave home for college, only to have them return home their freshman year pregnant with their hearts shattered and collegiate dreams sidelined. Our education liaison, Dr. Spivey, agreed to work with Marquita and Mrs. Drake and help them explore collegiate options. Her suggestion that they tour Miles College, a local HBCU (historically Black college or university), was met with guarded enthusiasm.

The next day, I got a phone call from Marquita and her mom. Raving effusively about Dr. Spivey's help, they shared highlights from their tour of Miles, expressed heartfelt thanks, and said they couldn't wait to start the application process.

Her acceptance was almost immediate, and she plunged into college life with glee. She moved into the dorm and made the honors list her first semester, which led to her being recruited to serve as an honors ambassador for the college, a rare thing for a freshman. Next, she ran for and was elected Miss L. H. Pitts Hall, a first for a freshman, which made her part of the homecoming court. Her collegiate triumphs kept coming—honors ambassador, a fixture on the dean's list, membership in two elite campus organizations, "crossing over" into a Divine Nine Black Greek letter sorority, and captain of the varsity cheerleader squad. Every time she invited us to an induction ceremony or game, I was ecstatic. But never more so than when Marquita invited me to attend her commencement exercise and followed up that triumph with the following text a few weeks later: "I received Board approval and have been officially hired as a teacher in the Jefferson County School System!"

This terrific young lady has become a trailblazer and role model for so many. She is the one of the first in her family to go to college and has broken her family's pattern of teen single motherhood.

Now in her second year as a teacher, Marquita has set her sights on pursuing post-graduate studies.

It's amazing what happens when a child has a chance to learn in peace and is encouraged to excel.

Chapter Fourteen

Nurturing

Maranathan Academy exists to give critically at-risk youth the intense advocacy, encouragement, and protection needed to survive living with persons who often bombard them with neglect instead of showering them with love. The Academy makes it possible for CAW students to be nurtured and have a family—when the families to which they were born reject them.

Victor

"Miss Dukes, all I want to do is see this boy get his diploma," said the feeble voice of Mr. Collins, a frail elderly gentleman, as he gestured toward the young man sitting beside him in my office—his grandson, Victor.

Sporting a thick, matted afro that looked as if it hadn't seen a hair pick in months, Victor sat slumped in a defeated posture, head down, hands clasped and dangling between his knees, not saying a word.

Mr. Collins handed me a folder and explained that Victor, an eleventh-grader, had been expelled from the Birmingham public school system. The folder contained a transcript and multiple suspension forms detailing fights with students and a verbal altercation with the school principal that was deemed serious enough to be designated a Class III violation. Such a violation triggers a mandatory hearing that often results in expulsion. A report stapled to the Class III suspension form contained a summary of the hearing, and several things stuck out for me.

The principal referenced having "had enough," described Victor as "angry" and "aggressive," then went on to say he was "constantly late for school, intolerant of good-natured teasing from students, had no interest in maintaining a proper appearance," and clarified the last descriptor with the following insults, "his clothes are always dirty," and "he smells." She concluded her testimony by declaring, "He needs to go."

The hearing officer agreed and decided that the altercation had "bordered on violence" and "requires expulsion."

Putting the folder down, I asked Victor if he had anything to share about himself or the altercation. He gave a negative shake of his still down-bent head. So, I began talking with Mr. Collins to get Victor's backstory.

It was grim and included a family history of crime, incarceration, parental neglect, and dependency on government assistance. He had a complicated relationship with his mother that I felt was directly connected to his troubles in school. Ms. Jackson, Victor's mom, was the daughter of Mr. Collins. She was an attractive woman with a hideous parenting style that fluctuated between verbally abusing Victor and completely ignoring his presence—until she needed him to "get her some money" for her other kids.

Mr. Collins explained that, almost a year ago, he'd become aware that the already dysfunctional mother-son dynamic had disintegrated to the point that his immediate intervention was required. Victor had been totally abandoned by his mother for an unbelievable reason—her boyfriend told her to.

Ms. Jackson's boyfriend said he "didn't like" Victor and ordered her to "put him out" of the house. She obeyed.

Unfortunately, her actions didn't surprise me. In more than thirty years of working with critically at-risk students, I've yet to have a mother choose her child over a spouse or significant other.

Desires for sex and companionship often win out over maternal instinct.

What did surprise me was a twisted detail in the story that rendered me nearly speechless with angry disbelief. Ms. Jackson's boyfriend was in prison for armed robbery and drug possession. She had allowed herself to take and carry out orders from a man who, Victor or no Victor, did not and could not live with her. In the process, she'd shattered her child's heart.

Not given a chance to pack, Victor had left his mother's house and started living on the streets. He was sixteen, alone and homeless, which explained why his clothes had been "dirty," as well as why he had "smelled" and been "angry." Other than spending an occasional night on a friend's floor, the streets were Victor's only "housing" option. He had to sleep in alleys and underpasses, constantly watch his back, and was forced to get tough—fast. It would have been nice if someone at his school had bothered to get an explanation for his appearance and behavior instead of passing judgment.

Despite being cast aside by his mother, getting little food and even less sleep, Victor hadn't given up. He'd managed to go to school and make good grades, all while being mistreated. By day, he was taunted viciously by his peers and received scorn and punishment from school authorities. At night, he was harassed by police officers for trying to sleep in the doorways of businesses after they'd closed up for the day. The harassment forced him into the dangers and darkness of street dwelling. If I'd been in his position, I think I would have been angry too.

Victor remained on the streets until Mr. Collins learned how he was living. Stricken with cancer and undergoing chemo, the dedicated grandfather mustered enough strength to get in his car and look for his grandson—driving around for days until he found him. The two became housemates, and the quest to find a school began.

Deeply moved by Mr. Collins's recount of Victor's backstory. I turned my attention to Victor, whose head was still bent down.

"After hearing what you've gone through and seeing how much your grandfather loves you, I have only one thing to say. Welcome to Maranathan."

His head shot up, and a ghost of a smile flitted across his face. "What do you want to do after you graduate? Do you have a career in mind?"

"I don't know. I guess I'll just go and take up a trade. Like be a mechanic or something, so I can take care of my little boy."

Whoa!

"Little boy? How old is he?"

Victor told me his son was almost two, and I asked about the baby's mother.

She's kind of "some timey."

"Some timey" translated to moodiness and failing to provide consistent care and attention for her baby. Victor wanted to get a job and his own apartment so that he could gain custody of his son. That told me a lot. Quite a few people think that only teen girls have children to try and create the kind of families they long for—loving, stable, et cetera. Not so. Many teen boys do the same thing. When abused or neglected, they often father children in an attempt to create the loving, stable families they wish they had. Unfortunately, teenagers rarely have the insight to choose partners capable of giving love and stability to a child. So, they succeed in becoming parents but fail to attain the type of families they so desperately need and crave.

The meeting concluded with setting Victor's start date as the next day. He wrote down all the sizes needed to issue his school uniforms, and I gave him a school handbook along with a verbal review of its policies, including the dress code—no sagging pants allowed, belts required, shirts tucked into the waistband, and so on.

We also had a hairstyle policy. We'd had several hair-related incidents, including a fight where a large afro afforded an immobilizing handhold and one instance of a student trying to sneak in drugs by hiding them in his fro. All the male-identifying students were required to wear a "low" haircut (no more than two inches in length) as a safety precaution. Upon hearing this, Mr. Collins grinned and said, "We're going to the barbershop right now!"

When Victor entered the building the next morning with a shy but bright smile, several in our Maranathan "squad" were shocked. His transformation was amazing! The unkempt hair was gone. In its place? Closely cropped hair that lay in natural waves against his scalp. Erica, our Dean of Students and the most shocked squad member, looked at me and said, "He doesn't even look like the same child! I can't believe it!" Relatively new to Maranathan, it was her first time seeing the dramatic difference that can be made in a student's appearance simply by getting a haircut and wearing clothes that fit properly.

Despite occasional criticism of Maranathan's dress code—such as "uniforms stifle free expression"—I have observed that appearance significantly affects how students are perceived by others, as well as how they view themselves and behave. Uniforms reduce negative behavioral exhibitions, and tighter control is exerted over tempers, even outside of school. Once, one of my boys told me about arguing with a guy in his neighborhood. "Miss Dukes, I almost fought him, but I had on my 'good clothes' (school uniform), and I didn't want them to get messed up."

Victor settled into student life and, little by little, let us get to know him. Even though he was eighteen and a father himself, he was still a little boy who desperately wanted a mother and often asked our faculty and volunteers for a hug. I had to tell him it wasn't appropriate, explaining that if he asked the wrong person for a hug one day—especially while off campus, where no one from Maranathan would be around to explain the reason for his request—the lady in question would probably think it to be fueled by romantic interest, and he might find himself charged with sexual harassment. Or, I further explained, she might be offended to discover his interest was purely maternal and seek to retaliate in some way.

A look of confusion spurred me to share the whole "Hell hath no fury like a woman scorned" thing and that I was praying daily for him to avoid experiencing it. He understood and agreed to stop asking for hugs. Next, I met informally with our teachers and volunteers to explain how much receiving motherly praise and encouragement would mean to Victor. They understood and gave both in copious amounts, which thankfully sufficed.

Feeling valued and secure, Victor started talking about things he'd always wanted to do, such as learning how to give a toast to someone the way he'd seen done on television. He became a Maranathan Academy Ambassador, outgoing and friendly to all visitors except law enforcement officers.

Whenever one accepted an invitation to visit the school or was encountered on a field trip, Victor immediately adopted a tough look. His posture stiffened, and he wore an angry expression, belied by slightly trembling hands—a heartbreaking display of fear-fueled hostility. To him, police officers represented persecution and harassment. Not one officer had tried to help when he was living on the streets. Several he encountered had zealously kept the homeless away from businesses, inadvertently depriving the vulnerable populace of the safety afforded by well-lit streets. Seeing law enforcement officers brought back memories of the dangers he'd encountered in dark alleys and underpasses—dangers that required him to fight for his virtue and his life. The rest of our boys shared his fear.

I've made it a mission to help our students overcome mindsets of fear and hostility toward law enforcement officers. Thus, Victor regularly encountered police officers visiting Maranathan for career days or just to spend their lunch breaks. I wanted law enforcement to be seen as human and approachable.

It paid off.

One day, Victor let it slip that he wanted to be a law enforcement officer but thought he'd be able to make money faster as a mechanic.

An officer visiting for lunch had the joy of explaining just how quickly a person could get through the police academy. Victor was elated.

So was I.

Having friends, Maranathan graduates, and a cousin on the job in law enforcement, the joy I felt hearing Victor say he'd like to be in law enforcement was indescribable. It was beyond wonderful to see a young man go from hating all law enforcement officers to planning to become one.

Victor earned his diploma in December 2019, secured gainful employment, was granted custody of his son, and will soon enter the next Jefferson County Sheriff's Deputy Academy class. It just doesn't get much better than that!

Chapter Fifteen

Dismantling Dangerous Mindsets

CAW students often view the entire law enforcement field in a bad light because of the reprehensible actions carried out by a few of its members. That view is grossly unfair to the thousands of good officers throughout the United States and poses a danger to CAW students relative to attaining success and longevity.

The willingness or ability of CAW workers to acknowledge and dismantle student distrust of law enforcement officers (LEOs) plays a pivotal role in helping students succeed. That distrust triggers CAW residents to run when told to stop or to become angry and resist arrest when calm compliance is the safer option. An expeditious dismantling of dangerous mindsets is imperative. It is most effectively facilitated by CAW workers who understand that critically atrisk students of color, particularly those who identify as male, have more reason than most to distrust law enforcement.

At Maranathan Academy, three steps are employed to help our faculty, staff, and volunteers grasp the rationale behind the distrust of LEOs. First, I share an example from my time in high school; next, I distribute scholarly articles for review and discussion; and last, I shine a spotlight on good LEOs.

The Example

Two years after I graduated, two police detectives told the principal of my former high school that they were looking for a "light-skinned black boy who robbed a store." They then asked if they could photograph "all the light-skinned black boys" at school. He said yes and, without notifying any of their parents, pulled every boy deemed "light-skinned" out of class, lined the boys up in the hallway, and made them pose for front and profile photos, which he then gave to the officers to place in a book for "an eyewitness" to review. My mom, who was a teacher there, saw the boys being lined up and told the principal in no uncertain terms that he was violating their civil rights, but her words fell on deaf ears.

None of the boys were identified for the store robbery, but the police continued to use the "light-skinned book" in other cases. One by one, over the course of a few months, several boys in the book were arrested, tried as adults, and convicted for various cold cases, which sparked outrage and shock in the community—because the boys had alibis. Unfortunately, the alibis weren't considered credible due to being "parental, sibling, and peer sourced."

One arrest and subsequent incarceration stood out painfully. My friend Tim was a senior. A tireless rapper and dancer, he had solid plans to learn a trade, work by day, and try to break into the "rap game" on nights and weekends. Sadly, his alibi of being at home on a long-distance, three-way call backed by phone records and the word of his mother and two friends from out of state was discounted. So, with no fingerprints or recovered stolen items tying him to the crime, Tim was convicted solely on the testimony of an "eyewitness" who had picked his photo out of the "light-skinned book."

Tim was a model prisoner and earned early parole. But he was sensitive, almost painfully handsome, and could not cope with the horrors of sexual assaults, overcrowding, and violence he was forced to endure in the penitentiary.

He's never been the same.

The Articles

At Maranathan, distributing scholarly articles for faculty, staff, and volunteers to review and discuss has proven effective in providing texture to the validity of some of our students' distrust for law enforcement. Here are two scholarly articles to review when time permits, which I hope aren't found too inflammatory.

1. "Police killings and their spillover effects on the mental health of black Americans: a population-based, quasi-experimental study," Jacob Bor, Atheendar S Venkataramani, David R Williams, Alexander C Tsai; The Lancet; Volume 392, Issue 10144, 28 July–3 August 2018, Pages 302-310.
2. "'That's My Number One Fear in Life. It's the Police': Examining Young Black Men's Exposures to Trauma and Loss Resulting From Police Violence and Police Killings," Jocelyn R. Smith Lee and Michael A. Robinson, Journal of Black Psychology 2019, Volume 45, Issue 3.

Note: Article 2 mentions Critical Race Theory, so if CRT triggers you, stick to article one.

Cue the Spotlight

The negative actions of a few LEOs often get more attention than the plethora of good officers who genuinely care about the people on their beats and lay their lives on the line—every day. It's incumbent upon us to highlight the actions of good law enforcement officers at every opportunity.

Here are just two examples.

1. Birmingham, Alabama: Birmingham Police Department officer Michelle Burton stayed hours after the end of her shift to take care of a one-month-old baby girl who, along with her three siblings, had been found in an apartment with their father dead

from a drug overdose and their mother unresponsive but alive, also from a drug overdose.
2. Las Vegas, Nevada: A police officer and his wife adopted five siblings after their mother murdered their father and technically orphaned them.

Sharing examples like these helps dismantle negative mindsets about LEOs and might produce positive trickle-down effects. One effect might be a reduction in suspects exhibiting the type of "hostile behavior" shown on police body cam footage, which could subsequently reduce LEOs' ability to use such footage to "justify" inflicting violence on suspects. Another might be a reduction of officer-suspect verbal and/or physical altercations.

Wouldn't that be wonderful?

Chapter Sixteen

Providing Hope

Hope is a small word that packs a punch powerful enough to change lives. Unfortunately, it's almost nonexistent in the CAW—unless a resident finds a source of hope like Maranathan Academy. Resources of hope in the CAW must increase pronto! Because giving hope to critically at-risk students works! I've seen it!

Dull, almost lifeless eyes begin to sparkle with new light. Students break free from emotional and circumstantial chains, gain confidence to plan for the future, and achievements never thought possible become realities. All because of the addition of hope. Anyone who doubts its power should just ask Nathan.

Nathan

"Miss Dukes, my cousin is in trouble, and I need you to help him," James said, looking at me with an anxious expression.

He had only been with us for a few months and was one of my most ironic enrollments. He'd been expelled from public school for gun possession but had a decorated police officer for a mother.

"He's not bad like me." James continued, "I mean, he's bad, but he's not bad like me."

With that great recommendation, I agreed to interview Nathan. While pulling out a prospective student form, I asked a standard question, and received an answer I was unprepared for.

"What did he do?"

"He killed somebody, and he's got a capital murder charge."

What?! Oh, Lord! How do I get myself into these things?

"Did he really kill someone?"

"Yes, ma'am, but he didn't mean to, though."

"Oh, okay." As strange as it might sound, I totally understand that a person can kill someone unintentionally. My aunt killed her husband in self-defense. She never meant for him to die just to keep him from stabbing her.

Nathan's interview day arrived, and though unsure of what to expect, I was completely unprepared for the Norman Rockwellesque image he and his mother, Mrs. Wallace, projected when they walked into my office.

She looked like my favorite deaconess from church. Her hair was perfectly done. She wore tasteful mid-heel black pumps and had a large purse draped on her arm that I was sure contained at least one church service staple—chewing gum or peppermint candy.

He was slim, soft-spoken, and looked like a junior deacon, right down to the sparkling white short-sleeved dress shirt and black tie.

This is the boy charged with capital murder? You've got to be kidding me!

After they were seated, I asked Nathan to tell me about himself. He shared that he loved music and produced records and music videos. His mother added that he also loved movies, which prompted the three of us to swap favorite film titles briefly before I guided the interview toward discussing his present circumstances.

"How long have you been out of school?"

"I've been out ever since it happened."

"You mean when the young man was killed?" He dropped his head.

"Yes, ma'am."

"Did you mean to do it?"

His head quickly lifted.

"No, ma'am. It was self-defense. He was trying to kill me." Then he braced as though waiting for me to pass judgment on him.

I didn't. I just moved on by saying, "I understand. Tell me what happened."

His shoulders sagged in relief, and he began to talk about the night that changed his life. He'd been king of the school and the neighborhood—team mascot, pep rally star, the go-to DJ for parties, and more.

On the night of his eighteenth birthday, Nate was serenaded by the crowd during half-time, then led them in cheering the team to victory. Scheduled to DJ an after-party, he went to the parking lot but never reached his car. A group of boys, jealous of his popularity, jumped him and began beating, kicking, and stomping him. The attack was the culmination of weeks of bullying so intense that his dad had bought him a handgun, registered it in Nate's name, and taught him how to use it. As horrified onlookers watched, brave but outnumbered off-duty police officers working security for the game tried to stop the attack but couldn't. Somehow, Nate managed to pull his gun, stick his hand straight up and fire—once. He hadn't aimed at anyone but the bullet inadvertently hit the boy leading the melee. He died a few days later.

Nate was arrested and charged with capital murder, altering life as he knew it. The school that had called on him frequently and helped organize his halftime birthday serenade suddenly wanted nothing to do with him and suspended him pending a hearing to consider expulsion. All calls for him to DJ parties or mix beats stopped, and he received death threats at home and at his part-time job. During Nate's expulsion hearing, numerous witnesses, including the off-duty police officers from the game, testified on his behalf. Each said the shooting was self-defense. And each expressed the belief that Nate would have been killed had he not fired. Sadly, their testimony didn't sway the hearing officer, and Nate was expelled.

It was an agonizing decision for everyone in his corner but doubly so for Nate, charged with capital murder and facing the possibility of losing his life because he'd defended it.

I assured him and his mom that prayers would be said for the jury to rule justifiable homicide. An invitation to become a student quickly followed and was met with enthusiasm.

"I would love to be a student here! Thank you so much!"

After completing the enrollment protocol, Nate's mother made an impassioned request.

"Miss Dukes," she begged, "please don't tell anybody that Nate is here. The death threats have gotten so bad. The boy's folks have been driving by the house, and Nate had to quit his job because they started waiting for him in the parking lot."

With my assurance that our faculty, staff, and students would be instructed not to share information about him being with us, mother and son left, and Nate's attendance began the next day.

Delighted to be back in school, he settled in quickly and was repeatedly overheard saying, "Being back in school feels like the weight of the world has been lifted. I'm just so happy!"

Nate was a good kid with intelligence to spare and a wonderful spirit. He very quickly earned the same "star" status he'd enjoyed at his previous school.

His declared love of music turned out to be an understatement. He adored it—constantly created rhythmic melodies with anything on hand. A pencil and a desk were all Nate needed to make beats that had everyone rocking, wanting to get up and dance!

I utilized his skill when it was time to teach "The Twelve Days of Christmas" for our holiday sing-along. Though the students had been dreading this moment, Nate's willingness to provide a beat transformed the traditional carol into a hip-hop masterpiece. To this day, I wish we'd recorded it.

All was bright on Nate's horizon except for one cloud—his upcoming trial. I'd written a letter regarding his exemplary performance as a student, which was added to the volume of other

Providing Hope 89

support letters his attorney had secured from ministers, community leaders, and so on. There was nothing left to do but wait—and pray.

Soon, the week of the trial arrived. Nate's mother, my prayer partners, Maranathan's faculty, students, and I remained in constant prayer, stood in agreement for a justifiable homicide verdict, and celebrated with yells of victory when one was handed down. The verdict paved the way for plans regarding Nate's graduation and post-diploma pursuits to go into full swing.

Soon, he was wearing what he never thought he would—a cap and gown—and leading the processional down the aisle of the church hosting Maranathan's commencement. Later, when walking across the pulpit to receive his diploma, Nate stopped and told the audience, "I'm so happy! This is the happiest day of my life! I just want all of y'all to stand up and do something with me."

Oh Lord, what is he fixing to do?

"Everybody! Lean wit it! Rock wit it! Lean wit it . . . !"

The church loudly echoed with cheers and laughter as Nate led us all in the dance inspired by the Dem Franchize Boyz song "Lean Wit It! Rock Wit It!" Tears were shed, as well. Nearly everyone present knew the extent of Nate's struggle and that it was a miracle for him to participate in a commencement instead of being incarcerated or buried.

Now, a successful commercial truck driver, happily married, and the father of two adorable little boys, Nate still mixes beats and produces videos. In fact, when I needed music for my documentary film "STAND!: Untold Stories from the Birmingham Civil Rights Movement," I called him and asked if I could buy some music.

"Miss Dukes, I'm not going to charge you. Whatever you need you got it!"

I paid him anyway, filled with pride that music from one of my kids would be in the film—which, incidentally, went on to win a Telly Award and be shown on every PBS affiliate in the United States. Yay!

Giving Nate hope provided him with an amazing testimony and a hard-to-top CV. Expelled, charged with capital murder, shunned, and written off as a lost cause, Nate has become an inarguable success story and recently added clothing designer to his list of accomplishments.

Although Nate wasn't in a gang, the young man he'd been forced to kill was. So, Nate started a clothing line with messaging to persuade kids not to join gangs. He's quite a role model, delivers motivational speeches around the city, and regularly visits Maranathan Academy to talk with and encourage our students.

On his visits, Nate always talks about the day he enrolled and explains how discovering a school that didn't think he was "bad" and that believed he deserved to get a diploma changed his life. Then he expounds a bit on what his time at Maranathan meant and shares that, for a few hours each day, he'd been able to forget he was receiving death threats, had been charged with capital murder, and was awaiting trial. At Maranathan, he'd been safe and could just be a kid.

Nate always concludes his talks by pointing at me and saying, "You see this lady right here? Whatever she tells you to do, do it, 'cause if it wasn't for her, I would not have graduated high school or done any of the other things I'm being blessed to do now."

What a loss that would have been!

Brian

"Just because I failed the exam doesn't mean I'm not smart. I'm smart, and I don't know why I can't pass that test!" exclaimed Brian, a clean-cut, gangly teen sitting in my office with his mother, Elaine, and stepfather, Trent, my friend since childhood.

Brian was in his senior year at a public school and had failed the Alabama High School Graduation Exam (AHSGE) for the fourth time.

The AHSGE, called "the exit exam" for short, determined whether a student would receive a high school diploma or a certificate of completion, which was a big deal. A diploma represented mastery of the course of studies mandated by the State of Alabama. Earning one gave a graduate options, such as military enlistment or, upon meeting admissions requirements, college or trade school enrollment.

By contrast, a certificate of completion (COC) signified that the holder had attended high school for four years and earned the number of credits required to graduate but didn't possess the academic skills necessary to receive a diploma. COC holders had limited options.

Some two-year colleges accepted COCs, but only a few four-year colleges did. The military didn't accept them at all. To make matters worse, students with COCs were only eligible to receive financial aid if they could pass the U.S. Department of Education's Ability-to-Benefit Test (ABT). Unfortunately, most people who didn't test well viewed the ABT just as they viewed the exit exam, with anxiety and fear—subsequently failing it, too. So, even if a student could find a college that accepted COCs, tuition would have to be paid out of pocket, effectively prolonging or preventing the earning of a degree.

Brian knew all this and was understandably distraught. "The counselor keeps telling me I'm going to have to just take the certificate and get hired somewhere that offers on-the-job training—try to move up that way.", he said. Tears filled his eyes as he continued. "But I don't want that kind of job! I want to go to college and become a banker."

My friend Trent chimed in. "He's a good kid, Donna, a real good kid. Now, they're talking about he needs to just forget about college. But that's his dream! This has made me shed some tears."

Brian's earnestness alone would have been enough for me to try and help him. However, I had extra motivation, Trent. Beginning in the fifth grade and all through middle school, Trent—already able to bench press 300 pounds without breaking a sweat—and our friend Rickey Smiley acted as my big brothers and bodyguards; they kept me from getting beaten up.

I was a really nerdy kid. Every day, I would carry all my textbooks home, whether I had homework in them or not, just because I liked to read them. This made me very attractive to bullies. Trent and Rickey, now a nationally syndicated radio host, had kept them away. Only someone who has been bullied understands how much that means.

I had to help Trent's bonus son.

Dabbing tears with a lace-edged handkerchief, Brian's mother, Elaine, began speaking, "This whole thing doesn't make sense. He makes good grades. All his teachers love him."

The two men in her life nodded in agreement.

"I just don't understand!" Elaine concluded before falling silent and joining Trent and Brian in watching me expectantly. All wore expressions that showed they were genuinely perplexed by Brian's repeated AHSGE failures.

I wasn't.

Years earlier and despite the problems in our educational system, Alabama had begun requiring students to take the exit exam. It always struck my mother and me as quite hypocritical. We knew several schools were watering down the state-mandated curriculum, and students were not being taught on grade level.

Years earlier, while on a routine visit to the school of a little boy in Maranathan's tutorial program, his teacher had said, "Let me show you something," and handed us a textbook. "This is the textbook I'm teaching out of."

It was a sixth-grade textbook, but our tutorial student, Jeffery, was in the eighth grade. At our surprised looks, the teacher explained. "When I get the students, they're not on grade level. I'm not going to fail them and lose my job."

We were appalled but understood. Teachers received low marks on their evaluations if they failed too many students. Therefore, because they wanted and needed to keep their jobs, some teachers promoted students to the next grade, whether they were on grade level or not.

Years later, those same students, many of whom had not received grade-level instruction nor been brought up to grade level, were required to take a graduation exam written on the eleventh-grade level. That was why Brian and so many others like him from schools in underserved communities couldn't pass the exit exam. He was collateral damage of the unfair policies and educational disparities such schools are made to suffer.

Without sharing why, I assured the trio that I understood the cause and thought I could help, then turned my attention to comforting Elaine.

"It's going to be alright. Sometimes, kids just don't test well or don't have an academic foundation strong enough to score well. Whatever the case, we'll work together to get him graduated."

"Thanks so much, Donna!"

"You're welcome!"

"Welcome to Maranathan, Brian! Hang in there, and don't get discouraged."

"Yes, ma'am," he replied without much enthusiasm.

On his first day, as is our standard practice with new students, Brian was given a battery of assessment tests. Just as I thought, his test scores revealed he had not received the proper foundation in core academic subjects. An ambitious plan was created for Brian that involved him being enrolled in an onsite dual course of study. He took remedial and mandated courses simultaneously. This allowed him to earn the remaining Carnegie units (credits) required for graduation while shoring up areas of academic weakness.

Brian attacked the plan with the type of ferocity a linebacker displays while creating a hole for the running back during a championship game. The intensity of his studies led to a wonderful discovery. He wasn't slow; he just hadn't been taught. Subsequently, he realized that college was back within reach. The light of hope began to shine in his eyes. He was driven, relentless—happy.

Brian graduated, enrolled at my alma mater, Miles College, and entered the workforce, excelling in both arenas. And, on Mother's Day Eve 2016, I had the joy of seeing him, draped in honors regalia, receive his bachelor's degree.

It was just what I needed.

Even now, it's hard to believe, much less write about, but my incredible, precious, brilliant mom passed away in 2004 on Thanksgiving night. At the time of Brian's graduation, some twelve years after Mom's transition, I still dreaded Mother's Day weekend. My spirits were lifted as I attended his commencement exercise and a post-commencement celebration hosted by his culinary genius of a grandmother. It was a celebration flush with the kind of laughter-filled family hijinks Mom would have loved. We took tons of photos, and to this day, I'm not sure who had the biggest smile: his mom, Elaine, his stepdad, Trent, or me.

After graduating college, another of Brian's dreams came true. He was snapped up by a major bank and performed with such excellence that he snared almost immediate promotion to the managerial level and was moved to a branch in Miami.

I'm in awe of him! Here's a kid, told that he wasn't smart enough to get a high school diploma, should settle for a certificate of completion, and abandon his dream of attending college, who is now a bank executive, happily married to a wonderful young lady he met while in college. A few months ago, he added girl dad to his resume when he and his wife welcomed their first child.

Hope-fueled second chances produce fantastic results.

Chapter Seventeen

Making it Safe to Dream

Dreams have a prerequisite—hope. Only there's a catch. In order to have hope, one has to feel safe. In order to feel safe, one has to feel loved and valued.

In addition to the previously mentioned student classifications of trauma victims and intellectual refugees, Maranathan Academy welcomes juvenile offenders with criminal records ranging from drug possession to murder, youth and adults who quit school as early as junior high but now want high school diplomas, and members of the LGBTQIA+ community who are often persecuted simply for existing. Each of our students can recall a time when they felt hopeless and unwanted. Before enrolling at Maranathan, that is.

The Academy prides itself on serving as a fountain of hope and an educational oasis for all who want to learn in a judgment-free, spiritual, inclusive environment.

Surprisingly, even now in the 21st century, I still get blowback and occasionally lose contributors for welcoming LGBTQ+ youth and adults as students, faculty, and staff.

Awareness that some who support my assertion that cyclical dependency on government assistance must end also have set views regarding the LGBTQIA+ community prompts me to make a quick request. Please don't stop reading this book because Maranathan Academy has some students, faculty, and staff in the LGBTQIA+

community. My fervent prayer is that, regardless of any religious or ideological differences of opinion, everyone can agree that all human beings deserve to be safe, free from persecution, and given the chance to work and learn in an accepting, nurturing environment. I love that such an environment exists at Maranathan Academy. Mom described it as "a beacon light to the educational struggle of man." It was a lifesaver for a terrific kid going through a terrible ordeal.

Sebastian

The doorbell rang one day when Maranathan was still located in my grandparents' old house. Opening the door, I saw a petite woman in scrubs standing on the front porch, tears running down her face.

"May I help you?"

"I'm looking for Miss Dukes."

"That's me," I said, and she stepped forward.

"Miss Dukes, somebody told me about you and gave me your card, and they told me that you take anybody, and I need you to take my child 'cause they gonna kill him!"

Telling staff that I'd be outside for a moment, I stepped onto the porch, shut the door behind me, and said, "Tell me what's going on."

"Three boys jumped on him between classes and beat him so bad. He's in the hospital, and they're already back at school. They didn't get but three days' suspension!"

"When did this happen?"

"Last week."

"Where were the teachers?"

"Standing in the hall, watching. None of them tried to help him."

"Why did the boys beat him?"

"'Cause they say he's gay."

"Is he?"

She hesitated.

This time, I took a step forward.

"It's okay to tell me."

Silence.

I placed a hand on her shoulder and said, "It's okay. I accept openly gay students."

She sagged with relief, then squared her shoulders and said, "Yes, ma'am. He's gay."

"Okay. Now, let's get some information and see how soon he can start."

She told me her son's name, Sebastian. He was the light of her life and seemed to be in terrible danger.

"The boys say when Sebastian gets back to school, they're going to get him. I'm so scared! I think they're going to kill him!"

"You're right, they will, or they'll try really hard," I said with sad conviction and made plans for Sebastian to enroll when he was discharged from the hospital.

We had no time to waste.

Two weeks earlier, I had enrolled a young man—from the same school—savagely beaten for being gay.

When Sebastian started attending Maranathan the next week, something was immediately apparent to everyone. He was quite simply one of the nicest kids we'd ever met. Despite challenges that included a speech impediment, extreme shyness, and major discomfort in crowds, Sebastian was always willing to help teachers and his fellow students.

While becoming accustomed to Maranathan, Sebastian learned he and his classmates had common interests and obstacles related to music, food, and lack of money; Sebastian began to blossom. But he was uneasy about acknowledging or discussing being gay. We didn't push—just let him move at his own pace. As time passed, it dawned on him that no one would bully him or make him feel uncomfortable. Soon, Sebastian was joining conversations, smiling, and sharing his dreams. He loved animals and wanted to work in an animal hospital.

Finally comfortable in his own skin, Sebastian lost his fear of crowds and got a job at the local movie theater—a place that once held great terror for him after experiencing ridicule. He also discovered his true calling was caring for people, and he became a certified nursing assistant (CNA) after graduation.

These days, Sebastian's time is spent giving compassionate care to his patients during a seven to three hospital shift, while most evenings and weekends find him at home tending animals he rescues off the street. Anyone fortunate enough to spend time with him knows that humans and animals alike are blessed to have Sebastian in their lives.

Chapter Eighteen

Sharing Uncomfortable Truths

Life in the CAW doesn't allow for many illusions or flights of fancy. One bad decision can determine life or death, which means CAW students have to grow up fast. Sorrowful events are common. Celebrating academic milestones is rare. The sad truth is that my students go to more funerals than graduations.

Ninety percent of Maranathan's middle and high school students identify as Black teenage boys. When they first enroll, most tell us that they don't expect to live to be twenty-one. Their lack of expectations relative to longevity makes planning for the future seem silly. This keeps them from believing in their ability to succeed and effectively places them on the fast track to sloth, prison, or an untimely death.

I've found that only by being jarred out of that mindset do our boys allow themselves to accept instruction or plan for the future, which leaves me no choice but to conduct a somewhat harsh but necessary two-step intervention. First, I shock them via the sharing of some uncomfortable truths. Next, they receive lectures on education's transformative power. Then, to drive home its availability and the kind of success education can generate, I bring in speakers who started out in the same neighborhoods as our students and had similar or even more serious struggles.

The intervention is a tremendous asset to one of Maranathan's top priorities—to give our students hope and help them learn how to dream. Why make hope and the ability to dream top priorities? Because dreams provide the fuel necessary to work hard, attain goals, and break cycles. Sadly, the CAW has a shortage of dreams but an abundant supply of bleak conditions—poverty, overcrowded housing, pervasive violence, and the constant presence of drug dealers and drug users on the street and in homes. It's those conditions that make an intervention necessary. Though uncomfortable to execute, I have found intervention to be the most effective way to help CAW students break free from counterproductive mindsets and overcome tremendous challenges.

The Intervention

While acknowledging the truth of their struggles, I stress the following to our students. First, we cannot allow challenges faced in life to become excuses for failure. Second, a person armed with a good education, a strong work ethic, and a determination to succeed can overcome being dealt a bad hand. Therefore, we cannot accept or wear the victim badge. Third, all of our problems cannot be blamed on racism or being born into poverty.

Lastly, because our students need to be aware of the challenges encountered by Blacks and other people of color, I outline the following implied or actual realities—while being careful to stress that challenges should never be used as excuses for failure.

Blacks in the U.S. are disproportionately disadvantaged in several areas, as indicated by socioeconomic strata distribution data obtained from the 2020 U.S. Census, which revealed disturbing socioeconomic distribution actualities.

Whites in the U.S. have the following socioeconomic affiliations: 8 percent live in poverty, 59 percent are categorized as middle class, and 72 percent are categorized as upper middle class. This illustrates a significant difference between the middle and upper middle class socioeconomic categories for Whites. However, a more significant,

Sharing Uncomfortable Truths

even startling difference can be shown. Among Hispanics in the US, 17 percent live in poverty, 18 percent are categorized as middle class, and only 9 percent are categorized as upper middle class.

The socioeconomic classification breakdown for Blacks in the U.S. is as follows: 19.5 percent live in poverty, 12 percent are categorized as middle class, and, in stark contrast to the aforementioned ethnicities, only 7 percent are categorized as upper middle class.

As it pertains to wealth classifications, the Federal Reserve Bank's 2019 Survey of Consumer Finances took the approach of examining median and mean familial wealth, which yielded disconcerting results.

- White families have a median wealth of $188,200 and a mean wealth of $983,400.
- Hispanic families have a median wealth of $36,100 and a mean wealth of $165,500.
- Black families have a median wealth of $24,100 and a mean wealth of $142,500.

Perhaps the most shocking illustration of the disparity comes from two statements from the Institute for Policy Health's 2016 report titled "The Ever Growing Gap."

1. "Over the past 30 years, the average wealth of White families has grown by 84 percent—1.2 times the rate of growth for the Latino population and three times the rate of growth for the Black population. If the past 30 years were to repeat, the next three decades would see the average wealth of White households increase by over $18,000 per year, while Latino and Black households would see their respective wealth increase by about $2,250 and $750 per year."
2. "If average Black family wealth continues to grow at the same pace it has over the past three decades, it would take Black families 228 years to amass the same amount of wealth White families have today. That's just 17 years shorter than the 245- year span of

slavery in this country. For the average Latino family, it would take 84 years to amass the same amount of wealth White families have today—that's the year 2097."

A projection that Black families will have to wait two centuries plus two decades plus eight years just to pull even with White families in terms of familial wealth is bleak, to say the least.

If the information from the Institute for Policy Health's 2016 report wasn't alarming enough, our students are asked to consider this. The 2020 U.S. Census Survey of Income and Program Participation shows the net worth of households with a Black householder—the person who owns or rents the home—was $9,567 in 2017, while the net worth of households with a non-Hispanic White householder was $171,700.

Next, to give hope and emphasize the life-changing power of education, our students are shown the earning differentials between persons who possess high school diplomas, degrees, trade certifications, or who enlist in the military versus persons who don't.

According to the U.S. Bureau of Labor Statistics, the annual salary for a person without a high-school diploma is $27,040, versus $37,024 with a high-school diploma, $40,248 with some college sans degree, $43,472 with an associate's degree, $60,996 with a bachelor's degree, $72,852 with a master's degree, $90,636 with a doctorate and $95,472 with a professional degree such as law school or medical school.

The information makes quite an impact. Fifty-three percent of our graduates enroll in undergraduate or community college. The remaining 47 percent attend a trade school or enlist in the military—I push trade school and the military just as much as undergraduate or community college. In addition, being knowledgeable about earning differences helps our students understand the critical importance of staying the course and completing their education. And it shows them, in no uncertain terms, that education makes it possible to narrow socioeconomic disparities for people of color.

Shining a spotlight on the impact of education prevents CAW students from using poverty and race as an excuse for failure.

Removing sources for excuses is essential when working in the CAW, where graduating from high school is frequently discouraged and made to seem unattainable.

Last, I give our students the most painful truth of all. In many instances, Blacks and other people of color must be twice as good as non-people of color to be hired, promoted, or even given a chance for employment. Before anyone gets offended and screams, "Don't say that! You'll fill kids with hatred or give them a complex," please allow me to explain.

I follow the acutely painful truth with what I have found to be the two key reasons behind it. One is surprising, the other not so much. The first reason is that some intentional or subconscious challenges and discrimination will occur due to specific individuals viewing people of color as inferior simply because of the color of their skin. However, the second reason is that some of the encountered challenges and discrimination will directly result from the actions of a portion of our fellow people of color. Like it or not, too many of my fellow Blacks and POCs have fallen prey to the traps that lie within dependency on government assistance.

Consequently, a rapidly growing subset has been created in the CAW, one that exhibits the following negative behaviors and characteristics:

- An almost nonexistent work ethic
- Criminal activity
- An entitlement mindset
- Refusal to accept personal responsibility
- Disrespect of women and elders
- Uncontrollable anger
- Violence against each other, as well as persons outside of our race

In turn, persons with hiring power use the negative behavior described above to justify not employing persons of color, thereby making a large number of POCs pay for the actions of a few.

While uncomfortable and probably not politically correct to do so, I believe that acknowledging the existence of and examining the reasoning behind a painful truth is a critical part of counteracting it. Undoubtedly, it would be far more pleasant not to share uncomfortable truths with my students and to paint them a pretty picture of a problem and prejudice-free life, but I'd be doing them a disservice. Therefore, laying everything out and then offering some absolute truths is the way to go.

1. Far more people want to see us succeed than fail.
2. Just as non-POCs shouldn't judge an entire race on the actions of a few of its members, neither should we.
3. Even with all the challenges and pitfalls encountered, people fare better studying and working hard than sitting down and waiting to be taken care of by the government, churches, nonprofit agencies, et cetera.
4. Hard work pays off.

And throughout the year, I give my precious students encouraging reminders:

To my Christian or religious students—"In spite of, in the midst of, and while enjoying periodic reprieves from life's inevitable challenges—God is and always will be good."

To my non-Christian or non-religious students—"In this life, you will have a mixture of challenges, tragedies, and triumphs. Remember, life isn't always fair, but karma is real, and the universe rewards hard work."

The intervention and insight described above, combined with the courses of study offered at Maranathan Academy, equip CAW students with skills needed to break cycles and make history—starting from within their own families.

Emily

Emily came to Maranathan Academy as a freshman. She was a baseball fanatic who stood five feet ten inches tall and had a smile that could light up a room. Along with copies of the standard documentation—social security card, birth certificate, immunization record, and so on—her mother, Mrs. Sanders, handed me a stack of papers to place in Emily's file. A copy of a protective order was on top of the pile. Having seen my share, I was intrigued to see that Emily's contained a very detailed exclusivity clause. It banned the confirmation or discussion of her enrollment and matriculation with anyone other than Mrs. Sanders or authorized designees whose names were listed. The protective order also excluded anyone but Mrs. Sanders or the authorized designees from picking Emily up. It concluded by stating Emily was to have no contact with her father or anyone on his side of the family, listing ten known to reside in the state. Additional documents detailed court proceedings related to severe injuries Mrs. Sanders had sustained from her husband, Emily's father.

"Miss Dukes, if anybody calls up here asking about Emily, tell them you don't have a student named Emily. Please, we can't let her daddy know where we are. He said he was going to kill me."

"Mrs. Sanders, we will never tell him Emily's here. She'll be safe at Maranathan."

"Thank you! We've been through so much!" Mrs. Sanders said fervently before sharing that the injuries she'd sustained from her husband had left her unable to walk without the use of a cane or to stand for more than fifteen minutes at a time—which effectively ended her career as a chef and kitchen manager. She'd been awarded total disability, but even with food stamps, she barely had enough each month to cover food and utilities for her and Emily.

Still, they were glad to have each other and had thought themselves safe—until recently, when Emily's father found them. He'd attacked Mrs. Sanders again but was thwarted from killing her by Emily jumping him and beating him off her mother. They managed to escape and hide in homeless shelters until their social worker could match them with a pro bono lawyer to handle filing orders of protection.

Emily was a joy. She dove into her studies with a joyful intensity that impressed and delighted her teachers. Everyone was amazed by her ability to keep smiling despite the burdens she carried—serving as a caregiver to her mother, having one brother in prison and two out on parole who struggled to stay on the right track, a daily walk home past bullies and drug dealers who were fixtures on the corners of her housing project, and one more particularly time-consuming burden that was perhaps the heaviest of all.

Six times a year, Emily helped her mother painfully climb the steps of a bus so the two of them could take a long trip to an out-of-state penitentiary and visit her brother. Only after those visits did Emily's smile disappear, but even then, only for a few days. She was a real trooper—carried a full load of classes, worked part-time, and babysat two of her infant nieces five nights a week for free.

Her instructors, guidance counselor, and I warned her she had taken on too many responsibilities, but she ignored us. To Emily's way of thinking, her brothers' mistakes meant she was her mom's last hope. And she placed tremendous pressure on herself academically and behaviorally.

So, it was no surprise when Emily's grades started slipping or when staff detected the smell of marijuana on her. I called her and her mom in for a conference, brought in a crisis counselor, and started a dialog on the dangers of drugs and the futility of using them to try and escape stress and emotional pain. We pointed out that once she came down from her high, the same stress, problems, and pain would always be waiting to greet her, which meant she would have to keep getting high, and we suggested it would be better for her to learn how to cope via talking with a therapist and allowing us to pair her with a mentor.

Thankfully, she agreed.

To help address Emily's trauma over seeing her mom attacked, I asked one of our paraprofessionals to mentor her. The mentor had seen her own mother stabbed multiple times by a man who "loved" her. Therefore, she understood the helplessness felt by children of domestic violence victims, allowed Emily to take shelter under her wing—and became an invaluable sounding board.

Therapy sessions and the extra support from her mentor allowed Emily to regain her academic and behavioral momentum. She also began to share more about herself—revealing that she loved to watch cooking shows, dreamed of one day tasting chicken cordon bleu, and that her decision to become a geriatric nurse was borne from her time in the homeless shelter, where she met elderly people in need of medical care beyond what the shelter could provide. Everything Emily shared was touching, but for me, her most poignant and inspirational revelation was that if she could complete her course of studies, she would be the first person in the entire history of either side of her family to graduate from high school.

As incredible as it seems, even though it's the twenty-first century, there are still families in the United States of America that have never had even one member to earn a high school diploma.

As Emily's graduation date approached, her mother was beside herself with pride and joy that her baby would be the first high school graduate in the entire family. An additional source of joy was provided by news that her son's upcoming parole hearing would take place a few weeks before Emily's commencement exercise, lending hope that he might be released in time to see his little sister make history. Emily shared her mother's excitement.

His parole was denied. Emily was sad and angry. I understood but asked her to put herself in the shoes of the victim and his family. "If you or someone in your family had been hurt the way your brother hurt his victim, would you want the perpetrator to be released early?"

"No, ma'am."

"Then you need to understand how they feel. Just pray for them to have a change of heart and for God to give you and your mom the strength to wait patiently for him to come home."

"Yes, ma'am. I had never thought about it like that. I'll pray."

Senior week arrived, and so did the deadline for graduate candidates to turn in their guest lists. When Emily handed me hers, I began to chuckle. It was huge! She had way more guests than the number allotted per graduate, which was understandable.

Excited and extremely proud relatives were coming in from Florida, Georgia, Michigan, and several other states to witness what was, for them, a huge milestone.

Determined to seat every last aunt, uncle, and cousin of Emily's, I reached out to several seniors who didn't have many guests coming and asked if they would give their empty guest spots to Emily. They happily agreed, and on a day filled with sunshine and smiles, Emily received her high school diploma.

The church was packed. Not only were many of Emily's relatives in attendance, but all of her Maranathan Academy schoolmates, some members of my book club, and—beaming with pride from the second row—the couple who had sponsored her scholarship. When Emily's name was called, the audience erupted in a nearly deafening roar of yelling, whooping, and shouting. It was wonderful!

Soon, the traditional commencement recessional "War March of the Priests" began to play, and everyone filed out after the graduates. To their credit, her two brothers managed to hold it together—until they exited the church. As soon as their feet hit the top step of the church's porch, both men broke down in tears, dropped to their knees, and began to wail. "You did it, E! You did it! I'm so proud of you!" cried one brother. Her other brother choked out, "You the first one, Emily, the first!"

After composing themselves, they walked down the steps, found their little sister in the crowd, and grabbed her in a double bear hug. It was a full circle moment—one I felt privileged to witness. Three young men had turned to the streets to escape their father's violence but had lost their freedom instead. Two of those young men had been given the chance to re-enter society and, though struggling, had chosen to show up and witness an incredible triumph for their baby sister—and their entire family.

Challenges still loomed ahead for them. Self-destructive tendencies and systemic obstacles designed to derail their progress would have to be overcome. But on that day, all that mattered was a family having the opportunity to gather and celebrate what only some in the CAW experience—a high school graduation.

Emily immediately enrolled in a training program and became a CNA. She now works at a major hospital, is happy to have broken the familial cycle of dependency on government assistance, and plans to enter nursing school.

Chapter Nineteen

Recognizing and Rooting for CAW Categories

Over the years, I've learned that CAW students usually fall into two categories—the persecuted: victims needing a safe haven and the persecutors: troubled individuals needing a second chance or a last chance.

The Persecuted: Victims Needing a Safe Haven

Abigail

Teachers are supposed to encourage academic achievement and work to enhance a student's education, not make it an exercise in torture. Apparently, Abigail's public school teacher had missed that memo. Otherwise, I wouldn't have been in the process of enrolling her and assuring her mother, Mrs. McKinnon, that academic achievement is celebrated at Maranathan. My heart went out to Abigail for having been bullied by someone who was supposed to prevent bullying—her teacher.

"She kept telling me that I was too smart," Abigail said, "that I should stop reading so much. She made fun of me because I go to church all the time and don't go to parties."

Given that Abigail, affectionately nicknamed "Abby," had a minister for a father, a church youth group leader for a mother, and an IQ that could qualify her as a candidate for Mensa, one could almost understand her being viewed as an easy target by *teen* bullies. But for her sedate lifestyle and intellectual acumen to have incited the ire of a teacher was disappointing and, as I listened to an account of what she'd endured, infuriating.

Abby had a compromised immune system. Her teacher's constant bullying exacerbated it, and she began suffering numerous bouts of illness.

"When she gets sick," her mother explained, "even though she has a doctor's excuse and does all the assignments she's missed, this one teacher refuses to accept them and gives her F's. Her daddy and I went to the principal, but he said he couldn't override the teacher." The unjust F's and constant bullying from the teacher caused Abby to start having anxiety attacks, resulting in several trips to the emergency room and additional doctor's excuses, which the teacher ignored, which incited more anxiety attacks. Her parents felt they had no choice but to withdraw Abby and home-school her.

It wasn't working out.

"She's so smart! I can't challenge her enough. I want her to get to do what she's been dreaming of doing since she was in kindergarten—go to college. But I can't send her back to that school. That woman was killing my child!"

I assured Mrs. McKinnon that I would help Abby and that I knew just how she and Abby felt—and I did. I had been that little girl—ridiculed, bullied, and, in one instance, harmed by the very people who were supposed to protect me—my teachers. Once in middle school and several times in high school, I endured torments by teachers. One of my tenth-grade teachers sprayed me with pesticide while he tended to the plants that sat directly behind my desk in his classroom, refusing to let me stand in the aisle out of the way; another spread a vicious, blatantly false rumor; and another berated me for wearing dresses and heels, saying I looked like a teacher and should wear jeans and tee shirts, instead. In my junior year, the National Honor Society committee blackballed me due to my having protested what I considered an unfair and antiquated policy—unwed mothers were banned from being cheerleaders, majorettes, flag girls, et cetera, but the fathers of the babies were allowed to participate in sports or any other any extracurricular activity they chose. My challenge led to the policy being eradicated. Some of the school's "power players" never forgave me for that.

Abby enrolled, found solace, and excelled even more than we dreamed. At Maranathan, she was safe to learn, be herself, and soar. Abby's progress was so great, her appetite for knowledge so voracious, that she graduated early and entered a well-known historically Black college or university (HBCU) at sixteen. This caused me to experience déjà vu since I had started high school at twelve and entered college at sixteen.

Right out of the gate, Abby was a star at college. During her freshman year, she was tapped to be in the honors brigade, placed on the dean's list, and when a well-known celebrity visited the campus, Abby was chosen to introduce him at a special assembly. Her introduction was so outstanding that people stopped her after the program, with exclamations of, "You speak so well!" and "Where did you go to school?" I know all this because she called me the day it happened—excited to share her triumph.

"Miss Dukes, I told them that I went to Maranathan Academy, and you taught me how to speak!" Then she added, "Thank you so much for being hard on me and for making us do all that writing and give speech after speech! It is really paying off!"

I don't have any biological children of my own—yet. Nevertheless, I had a fabulous Mother's Day weekend in 2016. On that Saturday, I went to see one of my boys graduate from my alma mater, and on Mother's Day, I hit the road to attend Abby's commencement exercise. It was such a privilege to see her graduate magna cum laude and to know that she would be starting law school that August. She's married now with two kids and has received her Juris Doctorate—making her Maranathan Academy's second law school graduate. I couldn't be prouder.

The Persecutors: Troubled Individuals Needing a Second Chance

Joseph and Marco

Mrs. Stephens, the mother of the two young men sitting in my office, was a diminutive figure with large, brown eyes. Her two sons, Marco and Joseph, born only a year apart, had a very strong bond and were seeking enrollment. Mrs. Stephens explained that both the counselor and assistant principal at the boys' high school had told her she needed to withdraw Marco and Joseph because they had bad grades, repeatedly skipped classes, and had no chance of graduating "on time."

The described withdrawal recommendation is one of the things that upsets me most about the actions of some public-school administrators. In states where the compulsory school attendance age is less than eighteen, parents can be pressured to permanently withdraw children from school. Alabama is among those states. To make matters worse, in some cases, children are allowed to sign their own withdrawal papers—without parental presence or notification.

I'd like to think that the person(s) who created the policies and laws that make this possible did so, thinking to prevent truancy prosecutions against students who have disabled parents or guardians and are forced to quit school and work full-time to help support the family. However, the sad reality is that administrators often use policies like the one described to force students like Marco and Joseph into withdrawing via what my mother and I called the "annual purge."

Each year, "problem" students are bullied into signing "voluntary withdrawal" papers. The school can then record the student as "Leaving to pursue a G.E.D." This allows the school's dropout stats to remain low and its percentage of failing students to decrease, which sometimes prevents it from being labeled a "failing school." In other words, in the hands of administrators not dedicated to

Recognizing and Rooting for CAW Categories

student retention, legal "voluntary withdrawal" policies are used to the school's advantage.

When she taught public school, Mom witnessed things during the annual purge that broke her heart. While on errands to the main office, she would see children—many with tears streaming down their faces—begging to be allowed to stay in school. Some would have a parent or grandparent helping them beg for "just one more chance," only to have the principal or another administrator thrust "voluntary withdrawal" papers at them while coldly giving a one-word command, "Sign."

Marco and Joseph were "purged" students. Each had more days absent than present, horrible grades, and numerous disciplinary problems that included fights, bullying, and extortion, followed by beating if a student didn't comply. In short, they were persecutors. By all accounts, Marco had been the leader, but Joseph had been a happy follower and had participated in each violent, menacing act.

I decided to enroll the boys and noticed something disturbing while voicing the decision. Mrs. Stephens directed intense glances at her sons and me; each glance was different. She glanced at me with hope, at Joseph with love, and at Marco with fear. I sensed that theirs was a family in need of serious help. Help that would be welcomed by Mrs. Stephens.

Wrapping up the interview, I asked if there were any situations or activities we, the Academy, needed to know about. I felt honored when Joseph opened up and shared that he and Marco were deeply involved with a gang, prompting a surprising interjection from his mom.

"They gonna do right, Miss Dukes. I promise! They want to change; I know they do."

She explained that Joseph "Joe" was her "good child" but had been shot "not too long ago," and both boys had decided to change their lives.

I asked about the gunshot wound and if he was fully recovered or would need to be exempted from the athletic portion of PE.

"He got shot in the leg, and they couldn't get the bullet out. It still gives him problems sometimes, but he should be okay for PE."

I praised Joseph for opening up and, while Mrs. Stephens filled out enrollment paperwork, started conversing with the brothers about college and career aspirations. The conversation let me know that trouble lay ahead.

Glancing furtively at his brother, Joseph shyly answered my questions and said he wanted to be a mechanic. Marco, however, watched me with a sneer and, in monosyllabic replies, answered only two of my questions. Mrs. Stephens voiced embarrassment over Marco's behavior and concern over the trouble she felt he had led Joseph into but seemed to feel powerless to stop it.

As she spoke, I felt such pain for her situation. She and her husband loved their sons and worked tirelessly on minimum wage jobs to try and provide for them. Yet, both their boys were teetering on a precipice—for one frustrating reason. Though streetwise, neither parent knew how to set rules and boundaries that could silence the siren call of the streets that had entranced their children.

Joseph and Marco started classes, and within the first two weeks, Marco's behavior made it clear he wanted his education to come from the streets. He rarely turned in assignments and displayed major attitude when asked about them. He also angered easily, accused instructors of "disrespecting" him when they asked for homework assignments, and behaved threateningly anytime he perceived the smallest slight.

Joseph was somewhat of a contradiction. He seemed on the fence about school yet was quiet, respectful, and consistently applied himself to his studies. However, he exhibited one alarming pattern of behavior—rushing to "help" Marco anytime he said he had been "disrespected."

I recommended a psychological evaluation for both boys. Not surprisingly, their parents were opposed to the idea. Unfortunately, stigmas still exist against acknowledging or seeking treatment for mental health issues. And those stigmas cause so many kids and adults to go without therapy or medication that could help them

Recognizing and Rooting for CAW Categories

lead productive lives. I didn't want Marco and Joseph to be counted among them. Determined to try and persuade Mr. and Mrs. Stephens to let their sons be evaluated, I asked the deans and crisis counselor to attend a brainstorming session for the upcoming weekend.

Unbeknownst to us, as a game plan to gain permission for the boys to be evaluated was underway, one of the street gang leaders had decided to make a show of force.

The following Monday morning, Marco and Joseph's mother came to school and asked to speak with me. She explained that one of the boys' friends had been killed over the weekend, and Marco had been with him.

It gets worse.

Mrs. Stephens went on to tell me that Marco, Joseph, and five other friends had stopped "hanging" with the gang as much. So, the leader got mad and placed hits on the seven boys.

Later that day, I learned from Joseph that the gang leader had assigned a number to each of the seven boys, indicating the order in which they were to be killed. Joseph said that number one had "gone to the country to live with his grandmama," numbers two and three were hiding, and the boy killed the previous weekend had been number five on the hit list.

"What number are you?" I asked.

"Number four, so they really were supposed to have killed me before him."

Marco was number seven.

I, along with the deans, counselor, and faculty, decided that, at the very least, onsite counseling sessions for the boys should begin immediately. Thankfully, we had already placed them in jobs and urged both boys to "just go to work and then straight home. Don't go to parties and stay out of the streets."

Joseph said he would, but Marco just looked on with his trademark sneer.

The next week, I overheard the two of them discussing a birthday party set to take place on the upcoming Saturday and begged them not to go. I told them I had a bad feeling about it. Joseph seemed to take the warning to heart, but Marco waved it off.

It turned out to be a setup.

The boys went to the party with numbers two and three from the hit list who had mysteriously come out of hiding. After partying for a while, another friend said he needed a ride home. When they reached his street, an SUV cut them off in front, and another blocked them from behind. Suddenly, two groups of boys appeared on both sides of the street and opened fire, shooting the car to pieces. One of the boys in the car was killed. Miraculously, neither Marco nor Joseph was hit.

At school the following Monday, I asked if they now understood why I told them not to go to the party and why the dean and their instructors kept telling them to concentrate on school and stay off the streets.

Joseph said he understood, promised to "start doing what y'all say," and backed it up by throwing himself with gusto into his studies, going straight home after work, and staying off the streets.

Marco had a totally opposite reaction. He wanted revenge and said the ambush was a sign that he needed a better gun. Already on a slippery slope, things quickly went downhill for him.

He started missing school and, on the days he deigned to attend, displayed hostile, increasingly erratic behavior—culminating in his having what appeared to be a break with reality. In the middle of his math class, Marco stood and began arguing, yelling at, and threatening an invisible student. Despite gesturing toward the door and insisting "that mother****** in that chair over there" was "mean mugging" him, his tormentor was one only he could see. There were no chairs by the door.

Still, his parents refused to let us get him help.

That night, he set fire to the kitchen after his family went to bed. Thankfully, he was noisy, and they woke up in time to call 911. The police took him to the hospital, where, placed in the psychiatric ward for observation, he explained that he "had to burn the house up so we could be safe."

After being discharged from the hospital and declared fit to return to school, Marco continued to refuse to do assignments, became increasingly argumentative, and, on one occasion, displayed menacing behavior toward an instructor. Although we hated to do so, there was no choice but to dismiss him.

His brother's departure freed Joseph. He started actively participating in class discussions and became eager to attend all school activities, especially field trips, which led to some interesting situations.

Arriving to visit with some circuit judges and tour the county courthouse, the chaperones lined up the kids while I approached the guards manning the metal detector and explained Joseph's special circumstances. "We have a child with a bullet in his leg from an old gunshot wound. The metal detector will go off, but it's okay. He doesn't have a weapon."

The guard in charge of the detector looked at me as if I were joking.

"No, I'm serious. There is a bullet in his leg. The detector's going to go off when the student walks through, and I wanted to explain why."

At the guard's silent but disbelieving look, I continued. "We use a metal detector every morning on the students, so he definitely does not have a weapon."

The look on his face changed to a cross between "well-now-I've-heard-everything" and horror, but he let Joseph through without incident. We all had a big laugh on the bus ride back to school.

The next academic year marked Joseph's senior year, and soon it was graduation day. His family was wearing custom-made tee-shirts declaring their pride and relationship, "Proud Mom of the Grad," "Proud Dad of the Grad," "Proud Grandmother of the Grad," and so on. Joseph was looking forward to starting trade school in the fall and turning his love for cars into a career as an auto mechanic. Our faculty and staff saw a bright future ahead for him. Everyone was on cloud nine.

Despite our collective joy, the day was bittersweet. Joseph's commencement was also the last chapter in the saga of the "marked-for-death seven." They'd all met their respective fates. Three were dead. Two were in jail. Marco was still unstable but managed to work odd jobs—occasionally. Only Joseph received a high school diploma and moved forward. Only Joseph had broken free.

Bittersweetness aside, the commencement ceremony was beautiful. As everyone spilled out of the church and onto the grounds to congratulate the graduates, I spotted Joseph laughing with his family. Pausing to take in the sight of their joy—I gloried in the fact that there stood a child with a bullet in his leg but dreams blossoming in his heart, holding his diploma and beaming as he posed for picture after picture with a crowd of smiling relatives and friends.

Now a certified auto mechanic, Joseph is working hard in a career he loves and has broken the cycle of poverty and violence to which he seemed to have been destined. He's a model citizen, and every time I see him or his mom, a hug-and-smile fest ensues.

Chapter Twenty

Confronting the Unthinkable

The poverty experienced by many in the critically at-risk world sometimes causes parents to allow unspeakable things to be committed against their children. Sometimes, they even orchestrate the unspeakable. To this day, a situation during my mom's last year of teaching public school serves as one of the most gut-wrenching examples I've ever seen.

As mentioned before, Mom was brilliant. She had a bachelor's degree with a double major in chemistry and mathematics. She was certified to teach French and had a master's degree in guidance and counseling. Yet, at her last assigned school, she was relegated to teach ninth-grade science classes, which the guidance counselors always filled with the kids considered problem students—the ones with discipline issues and truancies. All had little or no support systems at home. She once asked to be assigned at least one physics or chemistry class, only to be refused and told she was "needed" in ninth-grade science because she was "so good with those kinds of kids."

Since I was still in college, Mom and I shared her car. When I arrived to pick her up one day, my customary hug and kiss on the cheek was met with this reply, "I need you to take me to Mary's house. I'll tell you why on the way."

What she told me left me speechless with rage. Mary, one of her smartest, sweetest students, had been "rented out" to a police officer—by her mother. Mom explained that Mary had been sad and withdrawn over the past few days. Mom repeatedly asked what was wrong, but Mary had refused to tell her—until that day. Fourteen years old and the mother of a beautiful seven-month-old baby boy, Mary was tall and mature beyond her years in physique, intellect, speech, and mannerisms, so much so that she was often mistaken for someone in their late teens or early twenties.

Through tears, Mary had explained that in exchange for giving her mother a certain amount of money each month, Mary had to launder and iron the officer's clothes, cook his meals for the week, and "keep him company" while he sat at the table to eat.

Although Mom questioned her about it, Mary insisted she wasn't being sexually abused. Mom didn't believe her but knew it couldn't be proved without Mary's corroboration. She also knew that even if sex wasn't part of the current "rental agreement," it was just a matter of time before it became one of the "services" provided. Mary also contended that the officer didn't know she was only fourteen—highly possible given her mature appearance. Still, that didn't make his agreement with her mother any less repulsive.

Mom offered to call DHR and received a loud, emphatic "No!" from Mary. She was afraid she might be separated from her baby. Mom told her that efforts could be made to try and keep that from happening. But she knew, just as Mary did, there was no guarantee a fourteen-year-old mother would be allowed to keep her baby with her.

"If you call DHR, I'll tell them I made it up. I can't lose my baby! He's all I got!"

Mom agreed not to call DHR and told Mary she would try talking with her mother, Mrs. Allen, while silently thinking first.

Some might question Mom's decision to try talking with Mary's mother first. That's understandable. People who don't work on the front lines of the CAW are usually only faced with simple life situations, those easily categorized as black or white, right or wrong. Front-line CAW workers, on the other hand, are routinely faced with life situations too complex to be clearly defined as right or wrong. In other words, front-line CAW workers understand that life is not black and white. It's filled with shades of grey. In light of Mary's refusal to consider cooperating with DHR, Mom thought it best to try talking to Mary's mom before going to the authorities. She understood the fear behind the refusal. So, we went to Mary's housing community and knocked on her mother's door.

"Mrs. Dukes, it's so good to see you! Hey Donna! Y'all both looking good!" exclaimed Mrs. Allen with a big smile.

"Thank you, it's good to see you, too!" Mom and I replied.

With the pleasantries over, Mom got right to the point.

"I'm sorry to just drop by, but something is wrong with our child. Mary's grades have dropped, and she seems sad and withdrawn. Even her body language has changed."

"I'mma get on her about that! She knows better than that!"

"Now, don't fuss at her. I think I know the reason. She wouldn't tell me at first, but I told her I knew something was wrong, and if she didn't tell me, I'd have to report her change in behavior to the counselor so that she could investigate."

Ms. Allen's eyes widened, her posture stiffening at the word "investigate."

"Mary says you've been able to find her a job where she's doing laundry and cooking for a police officer. Is that right?"

With eyes narrowed almost to slits, Mrs. Allen replied defensively, "Yes. It's good for her to have a job!"

"But she's so young."

"Yeah, but she big! She loves to eat, and that baby eats a lot, too!"

Mom rebutted by reminding Mrs. Allen that both she and Mary received food stamps and that Mary received WIC for the baby.

Mrs. Allen insisted it wasn't "enough" and that cash was needed for clothes and other items.

Mom volleyed with, "Why do you feel comfortable with Mary having this kind of job?"

"Because I had a job taking care of a man when I was younger than she is!" Ms. Vaughn yelled, then gasping at her admission, sagged back in her chair, the defensive posture gone. Without it, she looked almost as young and vulnerable as Mary.

Mom and I exchanged glances of understanding. Ms. Allen's comfort in "renting" Mary out now made sense. She was doing to Mary what had been done to her.

It was heartbreaking, but Mom didn't let up, couldn't let up.

"Look, you and I both know that Mary is a beautiful girl and does not look her age. But we also know it's just a hop, skip, and jump from cooking and doing laundry for a man to having sex with him. She's already got one baby, and I sure don't want her to have another one. Do you?"

"No, but she needs a job."

"Yes, she does, but it's not good for a woman to be beholden to a man. Mary needs to earn her money a different way."

Mrs. Allen simply nodded in agreement.

Mom promised to help Mary get a job when she turned fifteen, which was only a few months away. Then she laid down the law.

"You tell that officer that Mary is no longer for rent! She wouldn't tell me his name, but some of my former students are on the force. So it wouldn't be too hard for me to get it, report him to the precinct captain for having entered into an arrangement with a housing authority resident and her fourteen-year-old daughter, and then sit back to let the chips fall where they may. If I had my way, he'd go to jail!"

"Yes, ma'am! I'll tell him."

That settled, Mom turned her attention to helping Ms. Allen map out a plan for Mary that included completing high school and exploring college and career options. She also brainstormed with Mrs. Allen on how to bring additional income into the household. She offered to mentor and tutor Ms. Allen so that she could try to become a supervisor on her job.

With the immediate problem resolved and solid plans for mother and daughter in place, it was time to take our leave.

Ms. Allen's farewell wasn't quite as effusive as her welcome had been, but that was okay. Mary was safe.

In a matter of days, she returned to her normal, bubbly, studious self, and there was no fallout from her mother over the rental agreement being exposed. In fact, their relationship became much stronger.

True to her word, when Mary turned fifteen, Mom helped her get a job at McDonald's. Moreover, under Mom's tutelage, Mrs. Allen tried for and received a promotion to supervisor. Both mother and daughter's achievements were cause for celebration. Gone was the willingness to be subservient to a man in order to make ends meet. In its place was the realization that a woman with a strong work ethic, who uses her brain instead of her body, can achieve success.

Though proud of everyone involved, I practically strutted with pride about Mom. A generational cycle of the acceptance of misogyny was broken, all because of one home visit from Jacquelyn Bates Dukes, my mom, who, even after she retired from the school system, stood by to provide counseling and a listening ear to Mary and her mother.

PART 3
Essential Strategies for Successfully Working with Critically-At-Risk Students

Chapter Twenty-One

Defy the Entitlement Mindset

Many in the critically at-risk world possess a sense of entitlement that causes them to believe they should be given anything they want—money, jewelry, designer purses and clothes, even cars. When that doesn't happen, some resort to scams that range from simple to sinister.

Mrs. McMillan

Mrs. McMillan was the mother of three sons. The oldest was a Maranathan graduate. Marquise, the second oldest, was entering his senior year with us. He was a very nice young man who dreamed of being a "boss rapper." As is the practice with all of our students who aspire to be pro athletes or superstar entertainers, Marquise was required to pick a second career goal, and we crafted a backup plan. He decided on auto body technician, and everything seemed set for a smooth school year.

His mom, Mrs. McMillan, was a gifted hairdresser, able to braid intricate styles that brought in good money—when she deigned to work. She was likable and gregarious. However, dating back to her oldest son's enrollment at Maranathan, she always needed money and always had a "big problem." I felt sorry for her, guided her to various agencies that could help, and, against the advice of faculty and friends, gave her money out of my own pocket many times.

Mrs. McMillan sang praises about Maranathan and me to almost everyone she met: individuals who came to the school for on-site visits, people she met in the grocery store—everyone. "Miss Dukes is an angel. Always helping me, my children, anybody that needs it! I love Maranathan Academy!"

During Marquise's freshman year, Mrs. McMillan had been in a car accident. We were very concerned about her and rejoiced when she fully recovered and received a personal injury settlement. Alas, a startling discovery cut our celebration short. Mrs. McMillan had expensive tastes and quickly spent her settlement on a luxury car, designer clothes, jewelry, and fine dining.

Broke, she began asking for monetary assistance that exceeded what our partner agencies could provide—and was way beyond anything I could afford. Soon, she had another car "accident," quickly followed by another and another. It was as if she'd decided to have a series of accidents after discovering how lucrative personal injury settlements were for the injured party. Flush with cash, she continued to be one of our most vocally supportive parents until she had another accident and actually got hurt.

A week and a half later, Mrs. McMillan asked to have a conference with me.

"Miss Dukes, we're going through some hard times, and I'm having so much trouble with my neck from that last accident. And, we got to move, and we need to rent a truck, and we got to pay to get our utility bills cut on at the new place. So, you going to have to give me that money you got for Marquise's scholarship."

What?!

Apparently, Mrs. McMillan had decided to stop having accidents and hit me up for her child's scholarship money. I couldn't believe it!

"Mrs. McMillan, I'm sorry, but that money is specifically raised for the student's educational costs—tuition, uniforms, field trips, textbooks, everything. You know that."

"Yeah, but that's not right! You done raised that money for 'Quise!"

After nearly an hour of her demanding the scholarship money, me explaining I couldn't give it to her, and her rejecting my offer to secure utility help through my church, I had an idea. I would arrange for Mrs. McMillan to meet with Mrs. White, a Maranathan volunteer with expertise in finding funds for people in need. Mrs. McMillan agreed to meet with Mrs. White the following day.

Yay! Problem solved, right? Wrong!

Upon learning the utility assistance would be paid directly to the utility companies and that she wouldn't have to rent a truck because Mrs. White had contacted a friend with a moving company and secured his services for free, Mrs. McMillan refused the help offered and repeated her demand for the scholarship money.

"She's going to give you trouble. Watch your back." Mrs. White warned.

She was right.

In the matter of one day, Mrs. McMillan went from describing me as an "angel" to calling me the most "lowdown woman" she'd ever met. She told anyone who would listen that I wouldn't "give the parents that scholarship money" and wasn't "being fair." Next, she embarked on a campaign of challenge and harassment that included but wasn't limited to:

- Asking other parents to demand their kid's scholarship money
- Asking our teachers to resign
- Complaining that Maranathan's assignment workload was "too much"
- Accusing the dress code of being discriminatory

At one point, she called the police to the school and asked for an incident report. Mrs. McMillan claimed Maranathan's requirement that students' waistbands be at their waist to prevent "sagging" (waistbands on or under the hips) was unfair to Black boys.

It was ludicrous and made me think of an incident when my mom was still alive, where one of our students refused to adhere to the waistband requirement. His father was serving time in the penitentiary, so doting and overindulgent paternal grandparents were serving as guardians. His grandmother made excuses when Mom talked with her, saying, "Leo can't wear his pants like y'all want him to 'cause he got a condition. He so well endowed, he has to let his pants sag down."

Mom didn't miss a beat and replied, "Ma'am, if Leo's so well-endowed that he cannot wear his pants on his waist, you need to take him to the doctor because there is something wrong with him. While you're doing that, we will place him on home study so that he can work in comfort."

Leo was at school the next day with his pants properly on his waist.

Mom and I had laughed for years about the overnight cure of his "condition."

Undeterred, Mrs. McMillan continued her campaign against Maranathan but with little success. The other parents refused to demand their children's scholarship money raised for their children, and the faculty and staff refused to quit.

Frustrated over the campaign's failure, she started yelling at me from her car during dismissal time. She'd holler, "You better let go of that scholarship money before somebody hurt you!" or, "Be careful, Miss Dukes! You making folks mad!"

She was clever with words and managed to make the threat sound like a warning.

It went on for weeks. And nothing could be done about it until I received a chilling message over social media one Sunday night: "Donna, I'm going to blow up your school tomorrow. Or maybe it won't be tomorrow; maybe it will be another day. Or maybe I'll put a bomb in your father's car and blow it up when he gets in it to go home one morning."

Whoever was making the threat knew that Son came to the school every morning to ensure all the classrooms and bathrooms were stocked and clean. The person also knew that Son was very precious to me, the only parent I had left, and that he was a treasured part of our students' lives, serving as the only father figure for most of them.

I immediately forwarded the message to our attorney and to a friend in law enforcement. Both advised me to take it seriously and call the police. I did, and as a precautionary measure, canceled classes for that Monday.

I told Son about the threat and its suspected source, then suggested he not come to school for a few days. He refused.

"I'm not scared of any threats. We're just going to put our trust in the Lord. You be careful, though. There's something wrong with that woman."

I should have expected Son's response. He was the co-creator and leader of the Birmingham Civil Rights Movement's Selective Buying Campaign of 1962, no stranger to threats and totally fearless. Son actually confronted Birmingham's notorious police commissioner, "Bull" Connor, during a Birmingham City Commission meeting about the unfair practice of segregation. He was one of the only men, Black or White, to ever do so. Joining Son that day were Dr. Jonathan McPherson, Sr., U. W. Clemon, and Shelley Millender, Jr. During the meeting, Bull, who was famous for his flamboyant racism, had a heated argument with Son and told him to leave Birmingham if he didn't like the way he ran it.

Son replied, "This is my town just like it is yours, and I'm going to stay here—live or die!" Son had also frequently sat outside the home of John and Deenie Drew, where Dr. Martin Luther King, Jr. stayed while in Birmingham. Each time he guarded Dr. King, Son had a shotgun "at the ready" to defend Dr. King against the Ku Klux Klan.

His lack of fear had been a constant source of worry for my grandmother. She used to talk with Mom and me about some of the things she experienced as his mother during that time.

"Hello."

"Is your son home?"

"No, he's not."

"Well, you tell your son that we're gonna kill him, and he better get out of town!"

"I'll tell him. But it's not going to do any good. He ain't afraid of nothing, been that way since he was a little boy."

Years later, she could laugh about it, but when it was happening, she was scared to death that someone would kill him because he wouldn't back down.

With a role model like that, I knew there was only one thing to do about the threat. So, taking a page from Shakespeare, I decided to "screw my courage to the sticking place" and fight back.

I traced the origin of the social media page from which the bomb threat was sent, and I discovered it belonged to Marquise. Next, I reported my findings to the police, who contacted the FBI. To make a long story short, because several people in Mrs. McMillan's home had access to Marquise's computer, the FBI could not make a criminal case. Their involvement, however, got the message across that we would deal harshly with anyone who threatened our school, students, faculty, or staff.

We never received another threat.

However, Mrs. McMillan employed numerous ways to harass us, including on Marquise's graduation day, where she caused a scene so disruptive that security had to escort her out.

When I speak on the need for another revamp of the current system of government assistance, the drama Mrs. McMillan caused is often used as an example of the dangerous situations that can occur due to the sense of entitlement possessed by many in the critically atrisk world. I am not a policymaker, far from it. However, I'm convinced that an effective revamp should include these principles:

1. More stringent supervision and enforcement of the community service requirement attached to welfare benefits.
2. Hardworking recipients like Sam's mom from Chapter Three should be rewarded for their strong work ethic and receive services to help them attain their dreams, including matching

grants for home ownership, educational advancement, et cetera.
3. All recipients should be required to take classes on financial literacy, parenting, and building generational wealth.

Of course, these are just my opinions. I fully realize that the "how" of fixing cyclical dependency on government assistance is an extremely challenging problem.

Nevertheless, my belief is shared by fellow CAW servant Dr. Thad James, Jr., Executive Director of Unbound 216, a ministry "aimed at breaking the cycle of recidivism." In talking with Thad one day, I voiced my frustration with an individual who constantly tried to convince me that increasing welfare benefits would solve the poverty problem. This individual became angry when I insisted that the solution required more personal responsibility instead of giving out more money. Thad agreed.

"No, giving them more money isn't the answer. Education is the key. Think about it. When you release people from prison, provide them with a few dollars, and return them to the same neighborhood that created their criminal behavior, you can count on most of them re-offending and going back to prison. We've found in our ministry that by the time a person reaches the bachelor's degree or higher, he isn't going to re-offend. There won't be a return to prison for him."

Chapter Twenty-Two

Take Nothing for Granted

Maranathan Academy is blessed to have quite a few supporters who volunteer regularly and genuinely empathize with the struggles faced by our students. In nonprofit speak, an empathetic supporter who engages with a charity and its clients is considered a champion.

Marley

Anna was a Maranathan Academy champion with a precious eight-year-old daughter named Marley, whose heart was as big as her mom's. On days when Marley's school was out but Maranathan was in, she came with Anna to volunteer. Our students viewed her as a little sister, but a staff member questioned why I allowed an eight-year-old to volunteer, "It's not like she needs to be here; she doesn't have volunteer hours to fulfill like high school kids do. What's the point?"

I gently explained that Marley's presence positively impacted the lives of our students and hers as well. The staff member didn't seem convinced but let the topic drop.

At the same time, a new craze had hit America—homemade slime. Created with household ingredients, Marley had become quite proficient in making it, and on one of her days off from school, she came to give her Maranathan friends a slime class.

It was one of the most precious sights ever to see a little eight-year-old girl teach a group of teens, some of whom stood over six-feet tall and sported gang tats, how to make slime. Fascinated by how common ingredients could make such a revolting yet fun mess, Marley's students hung on her every word and meticulously followed her instructions. The slime class was a resounding success and provided an unexpected lesson.

After cleaning up, Marley joined the kids, and I helped Anna serve the snacks she and Marley had brought. While the group practically inhaled a marvelous assortment of cookies, granola bars, and chips, Anna and I chatted.

"Donna, do you guys need any of this?" Anna asked, indicating the leftover slime ingredients of laundry detergent, shaving cream, et cetera. "We've got plenty at home. I just picked these things up on the way here."

"Absolutely! Everything will be put to use. Thanks so much, Anna!"

As we continued to chat, I noticed a student watching us. His name was Billy, and he was a very troubled young man. A high ranking member of a gang, he was constantly being disciplined for acting out. As for his home life, he had a father who deserted him and a mother who took out her anger toward her ex-husband on Billy. Desperate for love and acceptance, Billy had been vulnerable to gang leaders who preyed on such desperation.

Before I could announce that Anna was donating the leftover slime ingredients, he approached us. "Miss Dukes, can I have that washing powder?" he asked, gesturing toward a box of laundry detergent.

"Yes, I was just about to tell everybody that Marley and her mom were donating the leftover slime ingredients to Maranathan."

"Ooh-wee!" he crowed. "My mama's gonna to be so happy to get this! We ain't got no washing powder." Smiling widely, Billy cradled the detergent like a baby and returned to his seat.

When the other students saw him with the box of laundry detergent, they began to crowd around and ask for the other

Take Nothing for Granted

leftovers. One boy wanted a can of shaving cream, another asked for bottles of water, and another for soap. Each left the table sporting a big smile and with a new pep in his step.

Anna was dumbfounded.

"Donna! What in the world?" she asked in a frantic whisper.

"This is what I've been telling you. Things many people take for granted are luxuries to our students." I calmly whispered back.

"I don't understand. Why?"

"Because the SNAP program doesn't allow for the purchase of laundry detergent, cleaning supplies, feminine hygiene products, and other daily necessities."

"You're kidding!"

"Nope."

I went on to explain that the federally funded Supplemental Nutrition Assistance Program (SNAP), once known as the Food Stamp program, was originally part of a Farm Bill and was designed as a "...nutrition assistance program..." for "low-income individuals and families" who meet specific eligibility requirements.

"Unfortunately, people on assistance have to fend for themselves when it comes to being able to have clean clothes or bodies."

"Good Lord!"

Anna's shock was understandable. I had been floored by the list of items deemed ineligible for purchase with food stamps—soap, feminine hygiene products, laundry detergent, paper goods including toilet paper and napkins, and more. If it wasn't edible, it was ineligible.

It's beyond outrageous and makes me want to carry an ineligible list around. That way, when I hear people speak disdainfully about the underserved not smelling good or licking their fingers instead of using napkins, I could whip it out and say, "Take a look at this list of ineligible items. How can people smell good or practice table manners when they aren't allowed to buy soap, deodorant, laundry detergent, or napkins?!"

Accepting the explanation for the kid's excitement, Anna moved on to an observation she found troubling.

"Food is certainly on the list. So, why did they practically inhale the snacks?" she asked.

Still whispering so the kids would not overhear, I shared that even though their parents or guardians receive SNAP benefits for food purchases, most of our students come to school starving.

"Why?"

"Because many of the parents or guardians exchange the SNAP benefits for cash."

"How?" she asked with a baffled expression.

"The EBT system allows participants in government assistance programs like SNAP to purchase eligible items. In exchange for cash, the parent or guardian arranges to purchase a disproportionate amount of groceries for someone who doesn't qualify for food stamps," I explained.

For example, the parent goes to the store with the "customer" and, using an electronic benefit transfer (EBT) card, purchases $80 worth of groceries in exchange for $50 in cash. The cash is then used in one or a combination of the following ways:

1. To purchase items needed for the family to be clean
2. To fund visits to hair or nail salons or both
3. To purchase liquor, weed, or both
4. To purchase clothes or other aspirational items for the parent, not the child or children

I used to wonder which person was worse, the parent or guardian who doesn't leave enough on the EBT card to feed their children, or the "customer" who preys on the natural human desire for basic comforts.

But, after learning of parents making do with less food so the family can have hygiene supplies, I figured it out. It's the "customer" who's worse. However, at the end of the day, figuring out who's worse cannot be the chief concern. Focus should be placed on the deficits suffered by children of parents or guardians who sell EBT benefits and receive reduced meal portions, imbalanced meals, or, in some cases, no meals at all—especially toward the end of the month.

Apprised of a new CAW area of struggle, Anna gathered Marley, and the two said their goodbyes and headed for home. Later that afternoon, my cell phone rang. It was Anna.

"Donna, instead of taking my usual route home via freeway, I drove through the neighborhoods around the school. It was a real eye-opener for Marley. She looked over at me and said, 'Wow, Mom, we are really blessed, aren't we, with where we live and what we get to have in our house?' I've been trying to help her understand that not everybody lives like we do and that she should show gratitude for what we have. Hanging out at Maranathan today got that lesson across. Thank you so much for letting us be a part of your work!"

"You're more than welcome, Anna! But it's I who must thank you for being the kind of person willing to come hang out with us and bring your little one. If you weren't, Marley would have missed the chance to learn what so many need to know—that having clean clothes, enough food to eat, and parents who care is a blessing."

Anna's phone call brought me joy, a bit of enlightenment, and confirmed my belief that the struggle to raise good kids transcends socioeconomic lines. I hadn't realized Anna was struggling to help Marley understand her good fortune.

Convinced that her struggle could help others, I got Anna's permission to share a synopsis of our phone conversation—and started with the staff member questioning the point of Marley's presence at Maranathan. Sheepish after hearing the synopsis, that staff member became Marley's number one fan.

Chapter Twenty-Three

Think Outside the Box

A large part of Maranathan Academy's success can be attributed to what I call "Mom's magic." Jacquelyn Bates Dukes entranced her students. She'd walk through classrooms, popping her fingers to a favorite Rod Stewart song. Or she'd delight them with anecdotes about music, for which she was passionate—Lena Horne's Live at the Waldorf Astoria album, Perry Como's Catch A Falling Star, Tragedy by Marc Anthony, and so on. She never wore her religion on her sleeve, firmly believed that one should not judge or look down upon anyone, and, most importantly, Mom thought outside of the box.

Through the years, I've channeled that magic when faced with unorthodox situations—especially the delicate ones that could go really wrong really fast.

Faith

"Faith, are you sick? You keep putting your head on your desk."

"No, ma'am," came the muffled reply.

"Then take your head off your desk and get to work," I said before walking into the next classroom to speak with a teacher.

When I returned, Faith was face down again.

"Faith! Take your head off your desk. Now!" Deciding to stand by her desk until she held her head up, I was startled by the dreamy, close-mouthed smile on her face.

Uh-oh!

"Faith, open your eyes."

She tried but could only open them to slits.

"Faith, you're high!"

"No, I ain't, Miss Dukes; no, I ain't!"

"Baby, you're sailing. What did you take?"

"No, Miss Dukes, I—"

"Yes, you are," I said, cutting her off. "What did you take?"

She hesitated.

"Tell me!"

"I asked my grandmama how come her skin's so pretty, and she told me that she smokes a blunt every night, and if I wanted my skin to be pretty like hers, I need to smoke a blunt every night, too. So, I got one from this dude and smoked it."

Oh, Lord!

Awareness of the unbreakable, no snitching code she and her family lived by made it pointless to ask for the dude's name in order to report him to the police. So, I focused on Faith and wondered how I was going to put the kibosh on her new beauty routine.

"Oh, Faith, I'm so sorry you've started smoking weed. Go back to sleep. You'll have to make today's assignments a part of your homework."

She complied, asleep almost before her head touched the desk. Now, it was time to call Faith's grandmother, Mrs. Roxanne.

Walking quickly to my office, I lamented that because she'd driven a friend to a doctor's appointment, it wouldn't be possible for the guidance counselor, my mom, to make the call. Before dialing the number, I said a prayer along the lines of "Lord, please show me how to handle this," then I picked up the phone, dialed, and thought about how much was riding on the call's outcome.

If we couldn't come to an agreement, I'd have to call DHR, which would break my heart. Faith struggled with anger management issues and had been expelled from public school for fighting. Maranathan was her last hope, and a DHR removal from her home might reignite the violent episodes that had brought her to us in the first place.

Despite my trepidation, I couldn't help chuckling as I waited for Mrs. Roxanne to pick up. Her skin was indeed pretty. Whether or not that was due to a nightly blunt, I wasn't sure. But there was no denying she had a nearly flawless complexion and, except for faint laugh lines, a face devoid of wrinkles.

"Hello," said a familiar voice.

"Hey, Mrs. Roxanne, it's Miss Dukes. How are you doing?"

"Hey Miss Dukes! How you doing, baby?"

"Blessed. I'm calling to check on something. Faith is high, and she said you told her that if she wanted her skin to be pretty like yours, she had to smoke a blunt each night. Is she telling me the truth? Or did she go somewhere and get high just to get high?"

"No, she's telling you the truth. I told her that. You see how pretty my skin is, don't you?"

I knew it! Faith hadn't lied, which was good, but now there was a dilemma. Mrs. Roxanne was a powerful ally—one I couldn't afford to alienate. Without insulting her or her beauty routine, how could I persuade her to stop Faith from smoking blunts?

Suddenly, inspiration struck. I said, "Yes, ma'am, your skin sure is pretty. But these children today aren't built like you, Mrs. Roxanne. They can't take what you can take. Faith is so high she can't even hold her head up."

"You know what, Miss Dukes? You tellin' the truth! These children ain't built worth nothing, are they?"

"No, ma'am, Mrs. Roxanne! You're right about that. They sure aren't!"

"Alright, I'm going to tell her to leave them blunts alone."

"Thank you so much, Mrs. Roxanne! I appreciate you!"

"You're welcome, baby!"

That night at dinner, I told Mom and Son about the crisis of the day, and they congratulated me for its handling.

Faith never came to school high again, and Mrs. Roxanne made a pledge to start leaving weed alone and kept it—for which Mom and I thanked God!

Neither of us would have wanted DHR to become involved unless absolutely necessary. Mrs. Roxanne was one of the only stabilizing factors in Faith's life, and we knew how much she loved her, that she had not been trying to hurt her, and had actually thought she was giving her good advice.

Faith needed as many stabilizing factors as possible due to her previously mentioned anger management issues, which were exacerbated by family trauma and a tragedy.

Her parents were in a passionate but violent marriage.

During her junior year, her much-beloved father was murdered in his auto shop, and his killers were never caught.

Soon after his death, Faith began to fly off the handle at students, seeming ready to fight, but then quickly calmed down.

Mom and I were concerned that one day, Faith would go off on someone who wouldn't know her outbursts were of the flash fire variety—scary but nonviolent and quickly extinguished—and that she would get hurt or worse. We had strongly urged her mother, Mrs. Nelson, to let Faith get counseling and take some anger management classes. She refused, saying she didn't want outside help. However, she agreed to Faith receiving on-site counseling from Mom, which seemed to be effective. The angry outbursts stopped, and the rest of Faith's education went smoothly.

She graduated with honors and happily entered the workforce. But we knew Faith had only begun to address her trauma-induced anger issues and encouraged her to continue counseling via the wrap-around services offered to our graduates. She declined, but we kept in touch. Mom and I celebrated Faith's every milestone, including a successful work history and no verbal or physical altercations.

Faith flourished for twenty years after her Maranathan Academy commencement—until she was murdered—by her mother.

Never in a million years would we have dreamed Faith's light would be extinguished by someone she loved and who knew what to do if she lost her temper. Although no one will ever know what really happened, here's the generally accepted account. Recently engaged and planning her wedding, Faith visited her mother's home. An argument erupted, and when it was over, Faith lay dead on the living room floor—courtesy of a bullet from her mother's gun.

Sadly, her story is bittersweet, giving both a painful illustration of the success that can be achieved by thinking outside of the box and the heartbreak that comes from losing a student who had made it. Faith's murder represented one of the most heartbreaking losses ever suffered of one of our own. I, along with our faculty, staff, and alumni, were in agonized disbelief. Only a few of us could handle attending the funeral. I wasn't one of them. The tragedy came only a few years after I lost Mom, and I just couldn't handle going to the funeral of a loved one. I knew that I wouldn't be able to bear looking at a coffin, knowing it contained the body of one of my kids, which is how I view my students.

On the Monday after Faith's funeral, our faculty and staff gathered and tried to console each other. Through tears and laughter, we fondly swapped anecdotes about the wonderful girl we'd been blessed to encounter. We reminisced about the time she told a joke that was so lame she couldn't stop laughing for almost ten minutes, the way people had leaped to their feet and shouted as she sang a solo when her sister graduated from Maranathan, and the unsolicited and unfiltered advice Faith once gave a teacher on mating techniques that had left the poor woman sputtering with embarrassment.

We also received consolation by recalling the wonderful things said about Faith in the news stories surrounding her death. She was a much-beloved employee, how excited she, her co-workers, and clients had been about her upcoming wedding, and that she was planning to fulfill her dream of becoming a mom.

Still, for Faith to have beaten the odds and attained success only to die at the hands of her mother was beyond heartbreaking; it was disheartening. One of our staff asked, "What's the point of working with these kids if they're going to end up getting killed way down the road?"

It was a reasonable question.

When first told of Faith's murder, I, for a brief moment, wrestled with the sensibility of working to educate kids and help them gain distance or freedom from toxic relatives only to have them lose their lives at the hands of those same relatives.

Thankfully, after a bit of prayer, the wrestling match had yielded an explanation of the logic of our work, which I shared with my coworkers, saying, "I know it's hard to keep going after a loss like this, but we have to do it. If we don't, who will help these babies? So, let's thank God that Maranathan was here when Faith needed it, that instead of being pulled into a life of crime like so many of her relatives, she found love and experienced the satisfaction of having a job where she made a difference. Instead of dwelling on the pain of losing her, let's focus on her hard-earned victories and rejoice that for twenty years after high school, she got to enjoy life in a way she would never have been able to without Maranathan Academy. In other words, let's do what Mom would do if she were here with us—feel the heartbreak, but keep working."

That's what Faith and Mom would have wanted.

Chapter Twenty-Four

Require Improbable Peace

A vital component to successfully working with critically at-risk students is maintaining a peaceful, non-acrimonious environment. Without the presence of peace and civility, CAW students could easily revert to the chaotic behaviors exhibited or witnessed in prior education settings.

Peace is a must—no matter how unlikely.

Rasheed

Orientation for new and returning students was a resounding success. The post-orientation reception was in full swing, with people devouring hoagie sandwiches, chips, and the kind of buttery, luscious, lip-smacking, moan-inducing sour cream, 7UP, and sock-it-to-me pound cakes only a grandmother could make.

Helping at the serving table, I was smiling with contentment, completely unaware that a bombshell was about to go off.

Midway through slicing a piece of pound cake for the grinning baby sister of a new student, I was grabbed by the arm and spirited away by Ms. Moore, the mother of a returning student.

"You enrolled the boy that shot Rasheed!" she hissed as soon as we were out of earshot.

"I did? Who?!" I asked, horrified, quickly scanning the crowd.

"That boy over there!" She said, pointing with her free hand to one of our recently enrolled students, who was munching on chips while standing with his mom as she talked with another parent.

I knew that Rasheed, a returning student, had been shot—in the face, no less. What I didn't know was that our new student Carlos was the person who had shot him. Quickly saying a silent prayer for guidance to deal with a situation that had never been encountered at Maranathan, I attempted to console Mrs. Moore, who was still gripping my arm. I said, "Don't worry. The dean of students and I will handle this. Please calm down."

"Put him out! You got to put him out!" spat Rasheed's mom as she glared at the boy whose bullet had nearly ended her son's life.

"Ms. Moore, if I refused to enroll kids who have shot someone or been involved with guns, Maranathan would hardly have any students. And besides that, putting Carlos out might make him retaliate against Rasheed. I need you to trust the dean and me. Let us handle this."

"Aight," she snapped, using the slang for alright, before tossing her head and stomping off. She was still angry. No, angry was too mild an adjective. Ms. Moore was, as the saying goes, "hot as fish grease."

The next day was the first day of school. Before morning assembly, I called both boys into my office and, without preamble, looked at Rasheed and said, "I know you have beef with him because he shot you."

Next, I directed my comments to Carlos, "And I know you have beef with him, or you wouldn't have shot him."

Then, looking at both, I laid down the law, "Now y'all better listen to me real good. We will not tolerate any fighting, beefing, or even saying you want to fight. So, if you want to stay here and graduate, you will have to get along with each other. If either of you isn't willing to do that, you need to leave. Now." I let them think for a moment, and then I asked, "What do you say? Can you both be in the same school together and not fight?"

"Yes, ma'am," they replied almost simultaneously.

We never had a problem. Rasheed and Carlos actually became friends, and the display of their friendship provided an inspiring realization. With mutual effort and willingness to get along, even the fiercest adversaries can find common ground.

Chapter Twenty-Five

Fight the Stigma Against Mental Illness—Creatively

The stigma against acknowledging and seeking treatment for issues involving anger management, mental health, and substance abuse is an ongoing challenge at Maranathan. Although the negative behavioral exhibitions they cause are disruptive, anger disorders and substance abuse issues are at least easy to spot. Complex mental health issues aren't.

Sometimes, we work with kids for weeks before realizing they need help. Once the issue is discovered, we immediately notify the child's parent or guardian and, more often than not, encounter the same level of resistance shown by the parents of Reggie, the student who backhanded me, and Marco, the student who set his kitchen on fire while his family slept. Fortunately, that resistance to help is not always mirrored by the student.

When blessed to have a student willing to accept help, a blend of flexibility and creativity must be employed to allow for continued enrollment.

Constance

"My daughter Constance keeps fighting at school. I mean beating people down. She's just like I was back in the day. The killing part about it is sometimes she can't remember what she did to the children," said Manuel, whom I had known since he was fifteen.

He explained that the public school his mini-me attended was "thinking about" expelling her, and some friends told him, "Mrs. Dukes' daughter has a school."

"Donna, when they told me that, I knew I had to bring my baby to you. Your mama was the only one who could keep me from fighting when I got mad. So, I need you to take my baby."

Manuel was right. Mom had been the only teacher able to help him. And he had been one of her favorite students. An enrollment interview for his daughter was set for the next day.

Accompanied by his wife, Manuel entered my office and presented the apple of his eye, Constance. She was beautiful, tall, Rubenesque, modestly dressed, and quiet. Much too quiet.

As her anxious parents looked on, I tried to get Constance to talk about the violent behavior she was displaying in public school. "What's going on? Why are you fighting?" I asked.

Before she could answer, Manuel jumped in.

"They keep picking on her! 'Cause she's big like me and smart like me, and they are alley!" he said, giving a single handclap behind each of the last three words before continuing. "I didn't want to put her in that school, but it's the one she's zoned for. And I'm going to hurt somebody up there about my baby! I can't take it anymore."

"I understand, Manuel, but I need you to let Constance talk." Then, redirecting my focus to Constance, I asked, "Sweetie, why do you think you keep getting into fights?"

"I don't know. At first, I was walking away, like my daddy told me to, but then I just got tired and said if they want to pick on me, I'll give them what they're asking for."

"And what was that?"

Her face became animated. "A good old-fashioned butt whooping!" she said emphatically.

Yep, she's just like her dad!

Within a week of enrolling, Constance began opening up to us— sharing her likes and dislikes. She loved books, disliked "silly people," liked "old-fashioned dresses," and had a passion for cooking. She found special joy in baking cakes. Unfortunately, her family viciously discouraged her passion.

"You're already too big!" They told her. "You don't even need to think about food!"

To counteract their negativity, I encouraged Constance to bring her creations to Maranathan. "Go ahead and follow your passion, Constance. Cook! You'll have a school full of taste testers. I'll talk to your parents."

Armed with that encouragement, Constance became a veritable tour de force. She baked. We ate. And a dream of culinary school was born.

Being free to create inspired Constance to open up to us even more. She confided that she'd tried to kill herself, not once or twice, but on six different occasions. I asked if she'd gotten counseling, and she said no, which concerned me greatly.

Things went well until six weeks into her enrollment. Constance came to school dressed like a completely different person. Instead of wearing one of her customary ankle-length dresses, she wore a pair of skin-tight black jeans, and her usual ballerina flats had been replaced with six-inch stiletto thigh-high boots. Completing her new look was black fingernail polish, a ponytail hairpiece that hung past her hips, and makeup so heavily applied that it seemed she'd smeared it on with a spackle knife.

What in the name of God is going on?! I wondered but decided to observe her for a bit before commenting. Constance was walking and talking differently—speaking in a deep voice that was almost bass in pitch. And she was flirting with the boys, who were shocked by her behavior. Prior to that day, Constance had been too shy to even make eye contact with them.

By noon, I'd observed enough and called her out of the lunch line to stand with me in the center of the classroom while everyone else was gathered for lunch and structured game time.

"Constance, you look really different today, and you're not acting like yourself. What's going on?"

"Nothing!" she snarled, with narrowed eyes and a defensive stance.

"Is something wrong? Do you want to talk about anything?"

"No!" she snarled.

"Are you sure you don't want to talk about anything?"

"No!"

"What happened to the little girl who was here yesterday?" I asked.

A malevolent smirk appeared on her face. "She's not here today," came the same deep snarl but with a gloating tone added to it.

Uh-oh! "Okaaay. So, who are you?"

"I'm Candy."

"Ah, I see. Well, Candy, don't you come back tomorrow. I want Constance to come back. In fact, I don't ever want to see you here again. Understand?"

"Aight!" she snarled, then gave a derisive snort of laughter and went to get her lunch.

Maybe this is why she doesn't remember the fights she's had! I thought, hurrying to my office, eager to call Manuel and share what I'd discovered—Constance had multiple personality disorder (which is now known as dissociative identity disorder).

He answered on the third ring.

"Manuel, I'm so sorry to call you at work, but I've got news! I think I've found out what's been causing Constance's behavior problems. Brace yourself."

His response to the diagnosis was silence.

"I think that's why she's been getting into fights and not remembering them.

More silence.

"I just finished talking to someone named Candy."

"Oh, you just now meeting Candy?" he finally replied, sounding as if he thought my introduction to Candy was late in coming.

"Yes, I'm just meeting her! Do you mean to tell me you already knew Constance has multiple personalities?!"

"Yeah. But I told her when she gets to be thirteen, she's got to choose which one she's gonna be 'cause both of them can't be in my house!"

Stay calm! Don't scream at him.

"It doesn't work that way, Manuel. If Constance has multiple personality disorder, it has to be treated. She can't just choose the one she wants. We have a wonderful psychiatrist, Dr. Moha, who works with our students, and I can get Constance an appointment right away."

"That ain't gonna happen."

"Why not?"

"I don't believe in psychiatrists. All she's got to do is choose which one she wants to be. She can do that by herself. And we can help her as a family. We're gonna pray."

"Manuel, even though this is my first time working with a student with multiple personalities, I need you to listen to me. Constance needs psychiatric help. Now!"

"I am listening. I hear everything you're saying. But I'm saying that ain't gonna happen! I'm not taking my child to a psychiatrist! She is not crazy!"

I don't believe this!

"Okay. Well, thank you. Have a good day." I said.

"Alright, you too, Donna. But, hey! Have you met Cleo?"

"Cleo?!"

"Yeah. She's so bad that I told Constance if Cleo ever come back, I'm gonna put both of them out of my house! Cleo is something else, for real!" Manuel almost sounded impressed.

Shaken to learn that a personality worse than Candy existed, I ended the conversation and started praying—for guidance and for Cleo to never surface.

She surfaced.

Two months later, Constance was spurned by a boy she fancied, and Cleo decided to avenge her.

At that time, Maranathan was still located in my grandparents' old house. It had a marvelous old-fashioned front porch that looked out over a small yard, and we utilized it whenever the weather was nice. During a midmorning break on a beautiful day, Constance calmly walked out onto the front porch of the school, pulled a pair of scissors from her overalls, unfolded it, and threw it knife-style at the object of her affection while he stood in the yard below talking with friends. She missed, but as the group of students screamed and scattered, she reached into her overalls again. Fortunately, we managed to grab her and bring her into the office.

She grudgingly took a seat. Knowing that Constance would never have tried to hurt anyone and that Candy was more of an aggressive flirt and bully than a would-be assassin, I surmised I was dealing with Cleo. The supposition was confirmed when I asked if she had any more weapons on her. Cleo answered in an exhibition of startlingly fluent profanity—screaming, ""Motherf*****!"" and ""Da** bit**!""

I began to call for Constance, asking her to come back.

Cleo responded with even worse curses and started to rise out of her chair, but our counselor, who had experience working at an adolescent psychiatric facility, stepped in front of her. Speaking loudly over her profane litany, he said he would restrain her if she got up. She stayed put.

I continued loudly calling Constance's name, asking her to return. She did, slowly resurfacing with a confused expression that got worse when, at my gentle instruction to check herself for weapons, she found three more pairs of scissors, which she readily handed over.

Thank God! I thought, then called Constance's parents to let them know what had occurred and that she was being sent home pending a conference—the latter of which yielded mixed results.

Manuel and his wife agreed to let Constance have a psychiatric evaluation but refused to acknowledge or cooperate with its resulting

Fight the Stigma Against Mental Illness—Creatively

diagnosis. Constance did, in fact, suffer from multiple personality disorder. Her parents balked at the recommendation that Constance begin having weekly sessions with Dr. Moha—immediately.

The reason for the refusal? Manuel and his wife still thought Constance could "choose" the personality she wanted most. They truly didn't believe treatment was necessary. It was decided that Constance would be placed on home study, and I would consult with the board of directors and Dr. Moha on whether Constance would be allowed to remain a student. The refusal of treatment was disappointing, but there was one bright spot. I got Manuel and his wife to sign off on letting anyone on our staff, paid or volunteer, have "talk sessions" with Constance if I felt it would help her. Then, I begged Dr. Moha to become a volunteer staff member. He agreed, thank God!

Letters were sent out notifying parents, guardians, and supporters of the addition to our staff, and I counted it a small victory when there were no objections. However, there was no getting around the dilemma created by Manuel and his wife's refusal for Constance to receive traditional treatment. Although we used a weapons detector as part of our security protocol and all student bookbags and purses were searched before entering the building, having Constance at school could be too big of a risk.

Fortunately, after a follow-up assessment a few weeks later, Dr. Moha issued a report giving Constance the green light to return. He believed our students would be extremely considerate of her feelings going forward and that with the continuance of talk sessions between Constance and him, a repeat appearance by Cleo would be highly unlikely. So did I, but there were no guarantees.

The pros and cons still had to be considered. On the one hand, Constance was a very troubled child who would need to be monitored by a specially assigned staff member at all times—an added expenditure Maranathan's budget could definitely do without. On the other hand, I shuddered to think what could happen if we didn't try to keep her at Maranathan, where we could at least provide an atmosphere free from bullying and where Dr. Moha could provide therapy for her, albeit unofficially.

I had to try and keep her with us. She had such potential. She also had nowhere else to go. An unfinished, mandatory stint at the Birmingham systems's alternative school would have to be completed before she could return to "regular" school. And the alternative school operated on a point system based on good behavior, which neither Candy nor Cleo were capable of. Constance had only two chances for successfully completing the stint—slim and none.

Therefore, a return to public school was out of the question, and traditional private schools weren't options either. Her history of suspensions made her persona non grata. So, I made the only decision I could live with and kept Constance at Maranathan.

I spoke with each student and with every interested parent or guardian about Constance returning to school. I took the time to answer questions and gauge their level of comfort. The response was positive. Everyone I spoke with agreed that she should get another chance.

Our faculty and staff were great, too, and pitched in to help on what I called "Team Constance." Samuel, the counselor with previous experience from an adolescent psychiatric facility, agreed to monitor Constance, which worked out beautifully. He documented her behavior daily, and because he was familiar with her three personalities, could tell if Candy or Cleo returned. Our instructors challenged her academically while encouraging her pursuit of nonacademic projects, including cooking contests.

Regardless of the success Team Constance was enjoying relative to incident prevention and compliance with counseling, I was still concerned. There was no getting around the fact that the child's mind was housing three different personalities, one of which was dangerous. I was concerned she might break under the pressure—that either Candy or Cleo would overtake Constance and become dominant. The thought of that happening was horrifying. We had to find some way to help Constance emerge as the victor.

With my competitive juices flowing, I prayed, crafted a game plan, and cleared it with Dr. Moha. Each day, I made a point of taking a few minutes to focus on the way Constance interacted with others. I noticed that receiving praise and attention seemed to give her strength and confidence. Therefore, everyone on Team Constance increased the number of compliments we gave. The results were awesome! Our compliments of her culinary creations motivated her to attempt complex confections. Our collective praise of her academic prowess resulted in her submitting college applications. She felt loved, listened to, and supported, increasing her confidence.

Best of all, signs appeared that Constance was becoming the dominant personality. Cleo hadn't returned after the front porch incident, and Candy appeared only occasionally—usually after enduring a long weekend at home, where family members body-shamed her. Another good sign occurred one day while Constance and I were talking. Her body stiffened mid-sentence, and she'd turned her head as though listening to an invisible speaker. She then shook her head "no" and continued our conversation. I was thrilled and called Dr. Moha, who made comments that validated my excitement. He said the "no" head shake indicated Constance might be gaining control over the other personalities. I agreed and wondered how we could help her gain complete dominance.

It seemed obvious that to secure and maintain mental stability, Constance needed a place of her own so she could control the amount of time spent with her family. Therefore, an early graduation from high school was crucial.

Steps were initiated to place her in Maranathan's accelerated program, which included administering tests to determine the workload she could handle mentally, academically, and socially. Her scores were terrific, and I successfully presented the early graduation option to her parents—easing their concerns about her youth by pointing out that I'd graduated from high school at sixteen and that only after entering college had I found my niche and met people with whom I could relate. Once in the program, Constance seemed to establish complete dominance. Neither Candy nor Cleo ever appeared again.

Constance appeared to be firmly in the driver's seat, so efforts increased to prepare her to live independently. The first step was to counteract the body-shaming she continued to suffer from her family. I wanted her to embrace her power as a curvy young woman and introduced her to the art of Ruben. His work helped her begin to understand the power and beauty of being Rubenesque.

The second step was giving her magazines that celebrated curvy women, which resulted in her sharing that she used to sketch outfits.

"Start drawing again," I encouraged.

She did, and with help from a cousin who sewed, she began to wear her own designs and rock her curves.

The third and final step was enrolling her in a life management class taught at Maranathan. She learned basic life skills and was shown safe, affordable housing opportunities such as dorm-style income-based apartments in good neighborhoods.

Counseling and affirmations from Maranathan continued; when commencement time arrived, we threw a pre-commencement celebration for our graduate candidates. Constance, that year's class valedictorian, was the life of the party.

As everyone celebrated, I stood back and allowed feelings of joy to wash over me. Seeing Constance experience scholastic success, self-acceptance, and true happiness was wonderful.

After graduation, she enrolled in a renowned culinary arts program at a community college, earned a degree, and became a personal chef. By the grace of God, Candy and Cleo are still dormant, and Constance is confidently and successfully following her passions.

Chapter Twenty-Six

Understand the Importance of an Anchor Parent

The presence or absence of a loving, supportive parent, who I call an "anchor parent," plays a vital role in children reaching their full potential and largely determines whether they will enjoy lives of success, mediocrity, or failure in adulthood.

An anchor parent provides the love, stability, and encouragement children need to find their academic and social footing. In addition to mothers and fathers, anchor parents can be bonus parents such as stepparents, grandparents, aunts, uncles, cousins, or friends. Shared DNA isn't required, only love and the willingness to act as a barrier between the student and negative influences, including gangs, toxic relatives, or mercenary friends. Having an anchor parent is especially important for CAW students. Without one, many fall through the cracks. With one, they're able to soar to heights unknown.

Isaac

"Out of the night that covers me,
Black as the pit from pole to pole,
I thank whatever gods may be
For my unconquerable soul . . ."
- William Ernest Henley

Whoa! Go, Isaac!

The uniquely beautiful young man, with nearly perfect inflection, reciting the poem "Invictus," had come a long way. His classmates were enthralled, and I marveled at the difference between this Isaac and the one who had enrolled three months prior.

With Isaac sitting beside her in my office, his mom, Mrs. Oden, had made an impassioned request for him to become a student. "My whole family says I'm crazy, that Isaac's just stupid. They say, 'His daddy was stupid and wasn't nothing. So, he's stupid and ain't gonna be nothing.' But I don't believe that!" She continued, "Isaac's in special ed 'cause the school says he's slow. But when we're at home, if I sit with him, he understands all his lessons. I told the school, and they told me to stop trying to make him learn. His teachers say all he'll be able to get is a certificate of completion. One even told me to 'just give up' on him learning and start trying to get him a job moving stuff or cleaning up. But I love my child, and I can't give up on him. I know he can learn! He just needs a chance! Please help him!"

With that heartfelt plea, Mrs. Oden had sat back, reached over to grasp Isaac's hand, and waited for Mom and me to make a decision. Other than quietly saying "Hello" when he entered the office, Isaac hadn't said one word during the entire interview. He had simply nodded or shook his head "yes" or "no" when asked a question. Yet he'd listened intently, occasionally lifted his bent head, and with keen eyes and a shy, hopeful expression, had cast furtive glances in our direction. There had been something so sad about his silence.

Mom and I had accepted him immediately.

Convinced he couldn't learn and suffering from low self-esteem, it took us six weeks to get Isaac to hold up his head for more than five seconds—and another two weeks for him to maintain eye contact. He had been blessed with a beautifully deep ebony complexion, possessed an unconventional build, uniquely proportioned facial features, and had been made to feel ashamed of his appearance. Isaac was also very respectful and painfully shy. He never initiated a conversation but was encouraged to participate in class and share likes or dislikes. His replies were always given in a voice just above a whisper, "Yes, ma'am," "No, ma'am," "I'm not sure."

His mother, Mrs. Oden, was awesome, a true anchor parent. She was dedicated, loving, and fiercely determined her child would get the education needed to live his best life. From the time Isaac was in preschool, she'd given him daily affirmations, telling him he was smart and could learn. Sadly, her loving affirmations weren't enough to counteract the vicious words of teachers, students, or his own relatives who mistook his quiet shyness for stupidity and weakness.

Mom and I decided that we would gently but firmly require Isaac to learn and, subsequently, discover the extent of his capabilities. We honored his individual education plan (IEP) but pushed him further than its recommendations. We gave him assignments commensurate with his plan but also included some assignments that were at grade level and above, always with the caveat, "Just see if you can do these, Isaac. If you start feeling frustrated, you can stop."

He made B's or higher on everything, consistently gained confidence, and eagerly embraced new assignments—until he was tasked with learning a poem that would have to be recited from memory in front of the class. Isaac doubted the strength of his memory and was terrified at the thought of standing at the front of a classroom and speaking. We understood his fear but didn't exempt him from the assignment—just gave him a longer due date than that of his classmates.

Now, it was their assigned recitation day. Mom allowed Isaac's classmates a fifteen-minute practice session and noticed Isaac coaching several of them—pointing out missed lines or words.

He knew the poem!

Midway through the assigned orators, Mom surprised everyone by saying, "Isaac, do you think you're ready to recite the poem, or do you want to wait?"

He smiled wistfully but made no move toward the speaker's lectern, which was positioned next to Mom's desk.

"Come on, Isaac, just try. You can always recite it again on your due date. Will you try? Please?"

"Yes, ma'am," came his whisper-soft reply.

"Good! Be sure to say it loud enough for everybody to hear you." Hesitantly, he went to the podium, took a deep breath, opened his mouth, and showed out—proudly giving his audience a smile that rivaled the sun after delivering the last line.

From that day forward, Isaac embraced his newfound role as a scholar and walked like he owned the world with his chest out, shoulders straight, head held high. He was given a regular course load, routinely beat assignment due dates, and made A's—effectively resetting the grading curve and sparking good-natured competition among his classmates.

The change in Isaac was also evident at home, as his mother, Mrs. Oden, proclaimed while chatting with Mom and me one day, "Y'all, he's talking—in the car, at church, at the dinner table, everywhere! And when we get through eating and cleaning up, he says, 'I can't talk to you anymore, Mama. I've got to do my homework and keep my grades up.' I'm so proud of him!"

Junior year came and went swiftly. Isaac was thriving. He had a part-time job at a grocery store, was dating for the first time, and, to top it all off, he'd been offered an internship with the housing authority (HABD). But he refused to fill out the application. Mrs. Oden asked Mom to talk to him.

"I'm scared, Mama Dukes," he said, calling her by an affectionate nickname used by many of the students. "They want me to work in an office and wear a tie!" was his explanation.

"Well, what's wrong with that? You wear a tie at the store, at church, and for programs here at school, right?"

"Yes, ma'am."

"Well then, bring the application to school tomorrow and fill it out. We'll fax it for you."

He got the internship and did such a good job HABD kept him on part-time, which required him to leave the grocery store job—much to the sadness of his customers and co-workers.

Isaac's senior year was a triumph! HABD said he could become a full-time employee after receiving his diploma. His church made him a junior deacon, and—drum roll please—he was class valedictorian. In his valedictory address, Isaac thanked his mom for believing he could learn and never giving up on him. Then he thanked Maranathan for working with him, "pushing him." He declined the full-time position offered by HABD, choosing to remain part-time so that he could attend college and pursue a bachelor's degree in management. His pursuit was successful. One week after graduating, he was a fulltime employee at HABD and became lead manager of a housing community just a few years later.

There's more! Isaac went on to get a master's degree, is happily married, a homeowner, and is on track for promotion to upper-level management.

The game-changing impact of an anchor parent can only be matched by the destruction unleashed when one is lost.

Gerald

A phone call shortly after 2:00 a.m. jarred me awake.

"Miss Dukes, they killed Janice!" cried a frantic voice on the other end. It was Mrs. Warren, the parent of a former student.

"What do you mean they killed her? What happened?!"

"They killed her! I got Gerald and Shanté in the car with me right now. We're just leaving the hospital. Shanté says they're gonna get who did it!"

Gerald was a senior at Maranathan, and Shanté was his older sister.

"What happened?!" I asked again.

In a slightly calmer voice, Mrs. Warren explained that Gerald's mother, Janice Simpson, and Shanté had gone to the store and returned home. When Mrs. Simpson was getting out of the car, a boy walked up to her, shot her in the stomach, and walked away. Hearing a gunshot, Gerald ran out of the family's apartment and found his mother bleeding in the driver's seat.

"Who was the boy?" I asked.

"Shanté says she don't know who he was, says she didn't see him."

"Wait a minute! Somebody walked up to the car, shot her mama, and she didn't see him?"

"That's what she's saying."

A phrase came to mind that my mom often uttered when she heard unbelievable stories—*Anybody who believes that, stand on your head!*

Mrs. Simmons was taken to the hospital, where the surgeon assigned to her talked with Gerald and Shanté about the surgery he would perform, then let them go in to see their mother. They were relieved to find her able to talk a little and even laugh at a joke. It looked like everything was going to be fine.

It wasn't.

Mrs. Simmons died on the operating table, taking not only a beautiful spirit with her but also the last barrier standing between Gerald and toxic friends and relatives.

"Can I talk to Gerald?" I asked.

"Yes, ma'am."

Deep, almost guttural, sobbing was heard on the other end of the line.

"Gerald, I'm so sorry! Your mother was a wonderful woman, and I'm so sorry! Is there anything I can do?"

"No, ma'am. It's all my fault!" he sobbed brokenly.

"No, it's not! It's the shooter's fault, not yours!"

"No, it's mine!" he insisted.

"Listen to me. I know how much you and Shanté loved your mama. And I know what I'd be wanting to do if somebody shot mine."

Gerald got quiet.

"I'm asking you not to do it. Let the police do their jobs. Go home with Mrs. Warren and stay there."

Silence.

"Promise me."

"Yes, ma'am. I promise."

"Thank you! I love you, everybody at school loves you, and I'm going to call and check on you a little later."

"Yes, ma'am. I love you, too," he said.

Mrs. Warren came back on the line and said Shanté had asked to go to an aunt's house. We ended the call, and I started praying. Things were about to get bad.

Gerald was scheduled to testify for the prosecution in a contentious murder case. Only seventeen at the time, he'd played a major role in the crime but was granted immunity by the DA in exchange for agreeing to testify against two friends. There wasn't a doubt in my mind that his mom had been killed in retaliation for that agreement.

The DA's case hinged on Gerald's testimony, and since there was no way to be sure the murder of Mrs. Simmons would stop him from testifying, he was probably the shooter's next target. A wake or funeral would be a perfect opportunity for Gerald to be picked off. Keeping him safe would be challenging, and not just from a physical safety standpoint.

As one of the few Maranathan parents to hold a steady job, Mrs. Simmons had life insurance, a CAW rarity in my experience. Therefore, he would need double protection—from the shooter and from the toxic relatives trying to get their hands on his mother's insurance money. We had to keep him out of reach.

When I spoke to Mrs. Warren that afternoon, she said he'd cried himself to sleep and that Shanté and her aunt had called, wanting Gerald to come stay with them because "he ought to be with family." Mrs. Warren and I were pretty sure of their intentions, and she selflessly declared, "As long as I've got a place to stay, he's got a place to stay."

I thanked her and committed Maranathan to help provide food for her expanded household. I also promised to craft a plan for Gerald to safely finish school.

Not for the first time, I wished to have had earlier knowledge of Gerald's real backstory—that he'd been involved in the death of a young man he'd been beefing with over social media. It was as tragic as it was ridiculous. A social media feud led to a showdown between two sets of young men, one led by Gerald and one by the young man who was killed. All had once been friends. Because the young men in Gerald's group were eighteen, they were charged as adults. Understandably furious over his agreeing to testify against them, they'd vowed to "get him for snitching."

But I hadn't known. Gerald's mom had presented him as a dropout who'd just realized the importance of school.

After hanging up with Mrs. Warren, Maranathan's deans, several of Gerald's teachers, and I brainstormed. The following day, via a conference call with Gerald and Mrs. Warren, the deans and I presented a customized, accelerated graduation plan.

- Due to Gerald receiving death threats and word on the street that someone was "driving around looking for him," it was decided that Gerald would complete his assignments from Mrs. Warren's home.
- Dean Brown would pick them up each week to be graded.
- Maranathan's conference call line would be utilized to allow Gerald to attend classes and receive help from the guidance counselor when filling out college applications and Free Application for Federal Student Aid (FAFSA) forms.
- Ms. Tolbert, Maranathan's Dean of Students who once lived back east, found a college willing to accept him, then used her connections to secure a job for Gerald and a family eager to

Understand the Importance of an Anchor Parent

house him.
- Maranathan would hold a small private commencement ceremony for him and provide a plane ticket for him to leave for Boston immediately.

Gerald accepted the plan, and everyone celebrated. Mrs. Simmons's dream would be fulfilled. Or so we thought.

Two days later, ignoring Mrs. Warren's objections but promising to "be back in a couple hours," he went to visit his sister Shanté and didn't return.

Instead, he called Mrs. Warren and told her he was moving out. She immediately called me, and I called him.

"Gerald, what's going on? Why did you leave Mrs. Warren?"

"'Cause me and my family have been talking, and it's not right for me to go to college out of town. I've got to take care of my sister and her baby. Plus, we've got to handle some business."

"No, please don't do this! Think about what your mom wanted you to do with your life!"

"I am, Miss Dukes. I'll still go to college, just not out of town. My family made me remember how good I used to be in football, and they think I should go to a college with a football team so I can go pro."

What?!

He hadn't been on a football field in years, which I pointed out and told him to stick with his graduation plan, only to have him say, "But my mama told me I had to look out for Shanté."

"She meant years from now! Your mom never anticipated being murdered when you were eighteen years old! You're not even able to take care of yourself!"

He wouldn't budge. So, I backed off and tried to help in other ways. I reached out to the police and asked for heavy law enforcement presence at Mrs. Simmons's wake, funeral service, and burial.

God bless our brave officers in blue! They showed up in force—making it possible for everything to be carried out without incident. Sadly, in the weeks following, Gerald disappeared into the toxic world of his relatives. He stopped turning in assignments or returning phone calls, and backed out of his agreement with the DA. He also ceased cooperating with the detectives working on his mother's case and declared he and Shante would "handle it" themselves.

The well-made plan for Gerald's success was in jeopardy, and several Maranathan supporters called and sent texts, seeking ways to help. Most were still in shock that Gerald's friends had murdered his mother.

I wasn't.

There's a viciousness acquired from living in the CAW. Most of its residents see no way to escape or attain success. And life is only precious to people who believe success is possible.

Eighteen months later, Gerald resurfaced. He'd tried to "handle things" by shooting up the home of the boy believed to have killed his mother. It resulted in him serving a short stint in prison and struggling to find housing upon his release. His family was MIA. Their "love" and the fervor to keep him with them had evaporated as soon as the last of the insurance money was spent.

Via text one Saturday afternoon, he contacted me and shared his circumstances.

"I'm homeless. Won't nobody let me stay with them. Please help me, I'm broke."

I sent him some money and invited him to join Maranathan's Adult Diploma Completion Program (ADCP) classes so that he could finish school and receive more help through our wrap-around services. Gerald accepted—promising to be in class the following Monday. He never showed.

A few months later, I got another text from him asking for money. By then, I'd spoken with Mrs. Warren and discovered that Gerald was on drugs. Previous attempts to help individuals with substance abuse problems had taught me that there's a big difference between helping and enabling. So, I forced myself not to reply. Everyone from Maranathan who loves Gerald, is praying or sending good vibes for him to reach out again and be able to accept our help. If he does, we'll be right here waiting to place him with facilities that will provide counseling so that he can forgive himself and treatment for his drug problem so that he can have a successful life.

That was his mother's dream for her "baby."

Chapter Twenty-Seven

Create a Team of Champions for a Child

Many of Maranathan's students have endured serious traumas, some at a very early age. They still remember them, despite familial attempts to downplay the memories, saying, "You were too young to remember that!"

They weren't. I can personally attest to the endurance of early childhood memories. When I was twenty-one months old, my seventeen-month-old cousin Beverly flipped me off my Aunt Pat's lap, where I'd been happily playing. I remember it to this day—the feeling of terror as I hurtled headfirst toward the green carpet on the floor, my aunt's terrified scream, and Bev's look of indifference.

Aunt Pat's quick reflexes prevented injury and any need for counseling, but many children aren't as fortunate.

The majority of our students exhibit symptoms associated with post-traumatic stress disorder (PTSD) due, in my opinion, to subjection to ongoing violence, victimization, and familial dysfunction.

Research studies that explain PTSD's impact on students support that opinion. A 2019 study by Erica Gollub et al, analyzed exposure to traumatic events and symptoms of post-traumatic stress disorder (PTSD). The participants had witnessed violent crimes such as shootings, stabbings, and beatings, as well as experienced the murder of someone close. The results were alarming, with 45.7% screening positive for lifetime PTSD, 26.9% for current PTSD, and 21.2% screening positive for depression.

Equally alarming is the negative impact exposure to violence has on academic achievement, as evidenced in a 2020 article by Gerard Torrats-Espinosa, "when children take cognitive assessments in the days after a homicide has occurred in their neighborhood, their performance declines relative to other children from the same neighborhood who were not exposed to violence in the days before the assessments were given (Sharkey 2010; Sharkey et al. 2014)."

Environmental impact, along with past or present trauma, must be taken into consideration when working with critically at-risk students. I find that sometimes, memories of having witnessed a crime are so deeply ingrained it takes a team of champions to help.

Diane

Diane was a dynamo who stood at four feet eleven inches, weighed ninety-five pounds, and loved to be neat, try new hairstyles, make good grades, and dance. She had never been in trouble and had entered Maranathan as a freshman via a family dysfunction-based court referral. She had a great mother, but the drama-filled antics of relatives were a constant source of stress.

Diane was also a victim of bullying. During the enrollment interview, her mother explained that a group of girls at school kept "jumping on" and beating Diane because she defied their demands to stop turning in her homework, doing her hair, and "dressing cute." The tormentors outmatched her in number, height, and weight. But she didn't care and fought back. Inside her petite frame was the spirit of a lioness—one who refused to cower or hold her tongue.

Her courage was admirable, but something had to be done. What had started out as a group of three bullies had grown to seven, which horrified and baffled her mother.

"After she got jumped on so many times, I started thinking she was doing something to make them want to hurt her. When I came to pick Diane up the next time it happened, one of the girls was in the office waiting for her mama, too. So, I went over to her and asked. "Why do y'all keep jumping on Diane? What has she done to you?"

"Nothing," she said. "We just don't like her."

"Miss Dukes, all of them are supposed to go to the same high school next year, and those girls already have family there. I'm scared something bad's gonna happen!"

I enrolled her, and Maranathan's zero-tolerance bullying policy gave her a newfound feeling of safety. But other issues surfaced.

Diane barely ate no matter how much her mother pleaded, dropped into a fight stance if startled, always seemed to be in fight-or-flight mode, and was extremely cynical about families. We were very concerned.

One day, during the Academy's weekly rap session, the topic turned to losing family members to violence.

Diane joined the conversation, saying, "People thought I would forget what I saw, but I haven't. I remember it just like it was yesterday."

"What, sweetie?" I asked.

"Seeing my granddaddy kill my daddy."

Good Lord!

I'd known her father had been murdered but had no idea she'd been present or that her grandfather was the murderer.

"What happened?"

"They were arguing, and all of a sudden, my daddy pushed me behind him. Then I heard a shot, and he fell down. The ambulance came, but my daddy was already dead. And the police took my grandaddy to jail." She paused, then clarified, "He's really my grandmama's husband, but she makes us call him Grandaddy."

"How old were you?"

"Two, going on three."

"Did you get any counseling?"

"No, ma'am. Everybody said I was going to forget it, but I still remember it. Now it's time for him to get out, and my grandmama says we got to be happy when he comes home."

"Will you be happy?"

"No, ma'am, but I can't do anything about it."

Diane's matter-of-fact acceptance of helplessness was troubling. She was a fascinating blend of contradictions—feisty when standing up for herself against bullies outside of her family but not from within.

Diane also shared other traumatic circumstances during that day's rap session.

One night, an aunt assaulted her for refusing to babysit while she went clubbing.

Her mom had a foster child who flew into unwarranted, violent rages. It was like living with a human time bomb; everyone in the house walked around on eggshells. Diane's mom refused to cut ties with any of her toxic family members, and Diane waited fearfully for the next episode or argument.

The newly shared information explained a lot, particularly Diane's refusal to eat. Plagued by memories of past traumas and powerless to stop present ones, she was exerting control over the only things she could—what she put in her mouth and her mind. Ingesting only enough food to stay alive and displaying academic excellence made her feel in control while surrounded by the uncontrollable, but it affected her health. An intervention plan was needed, pronto.

I assembled a team comprised of a crisis counselor, guidance counselor, nutritionist, and several of Diane's teachers, then called an emergency brainstorming session. Together, we crafted a plan that was implemented the next morning.

Diane was sent to my office before first period. I shared the news about her new team, explained our concern over how little she ate, and then shared a personal experience from high school. Super busy with schoolwork, clubs, and the SGA, I often hadn't taken in enough calories. She thought it was hilarious when I told her my pediatrician had actually taken out his prescription pad and written a prescription for a popular candy bar: "Keep several bars in purse; eat minimum one per day."

"Do you like candy bars?"

"No, ma'am."

"Chocolate chip cookies?"

"No, ma'am."

Undeterred, I rattled off every high-calorie candy and cookie I could think of, only to be sweetly told, "No, ma'am."

Suddenly, memory struck.

"Diane, I just remembered something. My mom found a nutrition drink for me that came in four different flavors. Chocolate was my favorite, and I discovered it would get icy and thick like a milkshake if put in the freezer for a couple of hours. It was delicious! Would you try one if I brought you one?"

"I don't know."

"Please, Diane."

"Okay."

Thank God!

My multipurpose office contained a full-size refrigerator filled with snacks, lunch ingredients, and more. The next morning, I bought the nutrition drinks in each flavor and placed them in the freezer. During snack break, Diane came to my office, tried each flavor, and fell in love with chocolate. She took it back to class and drank the whole thing. Yay!

From that day on, I kept the fridge stocked with "Diane's shakes," and a routine was established. Before the start of each school day, she would come to the office, do a fridge-to-freezer shake transfer, return a couple of hours later, and take it to class, savoring it as she worked. Our counselor taught Diane some coping techniques, which helped her feel more in control of her life. She started to eat and gained a little weight. She was still tiny, probably always would be, but she was a healthy tiny. Her mom, Mrs. Lawson, was thrilled.

With concerns over Diane's health resolved, I was eager for Team Diane to focus on her career aspirations. She was now a sophomore and planned to be a cosmetologist, which is a fine career, but I was concerned about why she'd chosen it.

"Everybody says I'm so good at doing hair, I ought to go to cosmetology school," she'd once told me.

"Yes, you're good at it, Diane. You keep your and your mom's hair looking great. But do you like doing other folks' hair? And would you want to do other folks' hair for a living?"

"I don't know."

I suggested she look at some different careers and noticed her devouring material on nursing. She confided that she loved taking care of people when they were sick and had thought about becoming a nurse until some family members talked her out of it by saying that nursing school would be "too hard" and "too expensive." Wanting to deflect that negativity, I recruited a new team member—one who would spark ambition and show Diane what women could achieve—my good friend, Joan, a legendary local businesswoman.

She'd balked at my request, said she had no idea how to motivate kids, nor did she have enough time to volunteer in a "meaningful way." I explained that even five minutes could make an impact and was thrilled when she agreed to join Team Diane and visit Maranathan.

After meeting and shaking hands with each student, Joan noticed Diane staring at one of her rings and let her try it on. After Joan left, I learned that was the first time Diane had ever worn a ring, real or fake. She asked me its cost, was given a jewelry store's phone number, and returned the next day with a new outlook.

"Did you look up the ring?" I asked.

"Yes, ma'am, and I think I need to change my career."

Yes!

"Really, why?"

"I won't ever make enough money doing hair to buy a ring like that!"

"I don't know. Doing hair can be very lucrative if you have enough clients."

"Yes, ma'am, but that would take a whole lot of clients, and I don't want to do that much hair!"

Mission accomplished!

Diane sailed through the rest of her education, graduated with honors, became a certified medical assistant (CMA), and is working full-time in a doctor's office while attending nursing school. Her end goal is to become a nurse practitioner. We keep in touch, and I have no doubt she will make it. I can hardly wait to start planning my outfit for her graduation!

Chapter Twenty-Eight

Adopt a "Ride 'Til the Wheels Fall Off" Mindset

Perhaps one of the most important components of working successfully with CAW students is an unwavering determination to stay the course until they find their footing. I call it having a "Ride 'til the Wheels Fall Off" mindset. It has served me well in working with Grace, the precious girl who entered Maranathan Academy as a twelve-year-old expectant mother.

The Saga of Grace

Grace's struggle could serve as a textbook example of what not to do to a child. Though Grace's mom loved her children, she didn't know how to make them a top priority in her life or provide proper supervision. When Grace became pregnant at twelve, DHR removed her and her three sisters from the home. All four girls were placed with Sarah, a nurse and dedicated foster mother. She was happy to have them and looked forward to helping Grace raise her baby. For the first time in their lives, the girls had a stable home.

Three weeks before she turned thirteen, Grace gave birth to a healthy baby boy. Things were looking up until the unthinkable happened. During a routine court visit, the judge ordered the girls to be returned to their mother, Katrina, and for the baby to remain with the foster mother, Sarah.

Apparently, Katrina had been in communication with the court, pleading to get her children back because she'd "cleaned up her life." The judge bought it.

Everyone was in shock.

Two weeks later, she called the court and gave the girls back. Unfortunately, Sarah had been assigned other children, and none of the remaining foster homes would accept four children. The sisters were separated.

Although heartbroken over not being able to live with her son and siblings, Grace was willing to give her new foster placement a try. It was a nice, issue-free placement—until it wasn't.

"Miss Dukes, I went to the movies Saturday night," Grace said one Monday morning.

"That's nice, sweetie. What did you go see?"

I caught my breath when she named a movie that had just barely escaped getting an NC-17 rating.

"Who took you to see that?"

"Mrs. Martin's son."

"Why? How old is he, and who else went?"

"Thirty. Just the two of us. He said he just wanted to do something nice for me, and Mrs. Martin told me to go with him."

My reply of, "I see," was quickly followed by extracting her promise not to go anywhere else with him.

After Grace went to class, I called her caseworker to report what Grace had shared and received a troubling reply.

"Oh, I'm sure Mrs. Martin's son meant well, and she probably didn't think about how it would look for Grace and her son to go the movies alone. It was just a lapse in judgment. She's very nice."

"She may be ever so nice, but letting a grown man take a teenage girl to the movies is ridiculous!" I exclaimed. Then I asked, "When will she be able to go back to Sarah's?"

"She won't. Sarah's current placements are all long-term," came the matter-of-fact reply.

Things went downhill from there. It turned out that "a lapse in judgment" was not the only cause for concern regarding Mrs. Martin.

She also smoked weed, drank, and liked having lots of loud company who also smoked weed and drank.

A dedicated student, Grace had difficulty concentrating around so much noise. I contacted the caseworker again, this time requesting that Grace be given a new placement, which received a disheartening reply.

"Mrs. Martin is one of our best foster parents. She's just very social. Grace needs to adjust."

I expressed concern that if things got any worse, Grace might run away.

The caseworker said, "If she runs away from someone as nice as Mrs. Martin, she must have a mental problem, and I'll have her placed into an adolescent psychiatric facility."

Appalled, I called a friend who worked with Grace's social worker. She shared my concerns but was powerless to intervene.

One night after, an inebriated Mrs. Martin entered Grace's room, insisting she come downstairs and "be nice" to some of her company; Grace ran away. True to her promise, the caseworker placed her in a mental health facility where, at the time of this writing, she remains—due to fights with other patients and one escape attempt brought on by the desire to attend a birthday party for her son.

We who love her haven't given up. Maranathan provides distance learning, and the "village" that was formed shortly after she enrolled with us keeps her supplied with books, magazines, and any necessities not provided by the facility. Recently, I found an attorney willing to represent her pro bono. Hopefully, she'll gain her freedom soon.

Chapter Twenty-Nine

Accept the Fact that Sometimes You Will Lose

One of the hardest things to accept in CAW work is that no matter how hard you try, you're going to lose some students.

Billy 2.0

Case in point—Billy, the troubled young man from Chapter Twenty-Two. Remember the way he celebrated getting leftover laundry detergent during Marley's visit? How excited he was about his mother's anticipated happiness over receiving it?

That visit from Marley and her mom turned out to be bittersweet because it marked one of the last times Billy was in good spirits and behaving well.

His mom remarried, became even more verbally abusive toward him, and often forgot to pick him up from school or take him to his part-time job. Sometimes, she even forgot to feed him. She'd cook or bring dinner home for the family but forget to include Billy. He began to suffer from stomach issues.

True to form, when we asked that he be taken to the doctor, she forgot to make him an appointment. Thankfully, I was blessed to have a doctor friend willing to make a school visit and had Billy's mother sign off for him to get an exam. It turned out to be a common gastro issue that could be fixed with diet and an over-the-counter supplement. To Billy's sorrow, his mother forgot to buy the food and supplements, so Maranathan did it.

The forgetfulness continued, and with each neglectful incident, Billy started to seek comfort from his gang family—descending further into a world of violence and drugs. Acting out at school came next via his lashing out at the students, faculty, and me.

We were very concerned about him and started searching for a way to help him get back on track.

In true serendipitous form, I discovered an out-of-state law enforcement friend, along with a group of his fellow officers, had a weekend camp for troubled youth. They offered to give Billy a scholarship. Maranathan found a sponsor to cover travel costs, and the academic dean and I accompanied Billy on the flight. It was his first plane ride. He was seventeen.

Billy was a star at the camp. He earned honorable mentions for leadership, athleticism, and, best of all, good conduct. The weekend broadened his horizons and provided large doses of two things he'd needed badly—validation from and interaction with father figures.

On the return flight to Birmingham, Billy talked nonstop. Euphoric with pride over his camp accomplishments, he shared his plans for the upcoming school year. He promised to do all of his work, respect his teachers, "stay out them streets," graduate, and "join the service."

The euphoria lasted less than a week, thanks to his mother.

She and Billy argued shortly after his return, and during registration day the following week, he confided in Dean Brown and me about the argument. To Billy, the defining point was when his mother yelled, "I don't care what happens to you!"

Her words broke his heart and his resolve to "stay out them streets."

"When she said that, I said, 'F--it! I'm going to do whatever I want to do and go where somebody wants me!'"

Assuring him that his mom had spoken out of anger, we begged him not to abandon his plans. He just smiled—sadly.

Within two weeks, the old Billy was back with a vengeance, partying and getting into fights, devouring gun magazines, which were confiscated when he brought them to school, and cursing out his teachers and the school counselor.

We called a parent conference and requested permission to set up a psychiatric evaluation. His father was a no-show, but his mother attended. As was predictable for a CAW parent, she denied our request and said, "There's nothing wrong with Billy."

But there was, and things reached the point of no return during a field trip. Students were placed into groups and assigned to staff who chaperoned and provided transport. While walking with his group, Billy and another student began to loudly discuss the success of a well-known local drug dealer. When the staff member for his group attempted to re-direct the conversation, Billy screamed profanities at her and several times invoked the name of a powerful street gang. He was heard by a young man parked across the street, who got out of his car and asked for permission to talk with Billy. The staff member explained she couldn't let him speak with a student.

So, the young man stayed where he was and yelled to Billy, "Youngblood, you need to respect this lady! You don't know what you trying to rep. I was in that gang and ended up in the penitentiary. Please, youngblood, you need to stop!"

Billy cursed him out, too.

All of this was reported to me by the staff member.

Later, back at school, he continued to act out and threatened the life of his group's chaperone for "snitching on him," leaving us no choice but to suspend him. Once again, we requested permission to set up a psychiatric evaluation. Once again, our request was denied. Still wanting to help, we offered a special program that would allow Billy to work from home and possibly return to onsite classes later if an evaluation determined him not to be a safety threat. Billy was interested. He even said he'd be willing to talk to someone. But his mom refused and withdrew him, saying she would "find him a GED program."

It was hard to see Billy leave. All of us at Maranathan longed for a way to help his mother accept the fact that he needed psychiatric help. Sadly, we couldn't think of one, which troubled me greatly. Billy was awash in emotional pain and practically bursting with anger over his mom's emotional abandonment, so much so that he had become a danger to himself and others. My gut told me he'd explode one day and hurt someone or make someone hurt him. A few months later, I got a call that proved my gut right.

"Hey, Miss Dukes!"

"Billy! How are you? I've been praying for you. How's the GED prep going?"

"Not good. Miss Dukes, I need to come back to Maranathan! My mama was supposed to have called you."

"I haven't gotten a call yet, but you're welcome to come back. We just need you to get counseling. Are you and your mom willing to do that?"

"Yes, ma'am. Thank you!" he said tearfully.

"Billy, what's wrong?"

"I don't know! I just . . . I don't know. I just feel like don't nobody love me!"

"That's not true! I love you, and so do Dean Brown, Dean Tolbert, Mrs. Mitchell, and the officers at the camp. We all love you. You know that, don't you?"

"Yes, ma'am, but my family all mad at me cause the house got shot up, and my mama won't let me live with her no more."

Uh-oh!

"Oh no! Tell me what happened."

After hearing his account and expressing concern, I tried to encourage him.

"I'm sure your family loves you. Maybe they'll come around after you get some counseling, get back in school, and start working. We'll help you to get a part-time job. It's going to be alright. You'll see."

"Yes, ma'am. I hope so. I love you, Miss Dukes. My mama gonna call you."

"I love you too, sweetie, and I'm looking forward to you coming back."

"Me, too!"

His mother never called, so I reached out to her but received no reply.

Meanwhile, I heard some troubling news via the student grapevine. Billy was beefing with a dangerous group of boys. A few months later, his photo flashed on the screen during a local newscast.

Billy was dead—shot by one of the boys he was beefing with.

We knew we'd done everything we could to help, but Billy's tragic loss still cut deep for our Maranathan family. Just as we did when Faith was murdered, we decided not to focus on the tragedy. Instead, we gave thanks for the times we brought joy into Billy's life. Then, we had a special reflection time for the whole school and swapped anecdotes about his mischievous grin, contagious laughter, and almost encyclopedic knowledge of blues songs. One by one, we chronicled all the ways our lives had been enriched by having met, taught, and gone to school with a little boy named Billy.

Chapter Thirty

Remember Why You Serve

A fascinating mix of burdens and indescribable rewards comprise the CAW work experience. However, the joy of seeing students or clients change their lives and break destructive cycles isn't always enough to recuperate from a draining work week. We CAW workers often encounter resistance and rejection from the very people we're trying to help. When faced with such encounters, it's important to remember why we serve. We help critically at-risk youth and adults escape a world they never asked to inhabit, and we help them write a new chapter in their family's history.

My father, Son, always said, "If you see a fool, follow him home. Then you'll find out why he's a fool."

Obviously, he didn't mean it literally. Yet, truer words were never spoken. Students usually mirror their home environment. An anecdote once shared by the late John Wright, a dear friend and champion for the underserved, provides the perfect illustration.

"I volunteer a lot at homeless shelters. I get to know the men there pretty well. I was speaking to one of the gentlemen and asked how he came to become homeless. He explained, 'Everybody in my house was an alcoholic. I swore I'd never be like them. Every day, I went to school and came back home to a house full of drunks. I quit school, got a job, but didn't move out. I still came back every day to a house full of drunks. So, I moved out, tried to live on my own a couple of times, but I always came back, and everybody was still drunk. Eventually, I gave up, and I became what was in the house.'"

That's why it's so important for Maranathan Academy and other CAW organizations to exist. Our work helps keep critically at-risk individuals from becoming or continuing to be "what's in the house."

When I speak to groups about the importance of helping CAW students change their trajectory, I often start with John's anecdote and conclude with an illustration of success borne of dogged determination to keep a child from becoming what was "in the house."

Lil' Man

Just like my mom, Son had friends from all walks of life. Many years ago, one of them ran a "house of ill repute" where he sold liquor, hosted illegal gambling, and, because he rented rooms by the hour, kept a "stable" of prostitutes onsite. Son's friend was a rascal, but he had a grandson affectionately called Lil' Man whom he loved with all his heart and was raising on his own.

He feared Lil' Man would follow in his footsteps and wanted him to have a different kind of life. He decided to "put him in school early" by enrolling him in a local church's kindergarten (pre-school in modern speak). He was three years old.

Lil' Man's first day of school started off great. He was smart, cute as a button, and full of personality. Everything went smoothly until lunchtime.

He was skipped over as the lunches were passed out. His teacher and her aide were the servers and somehow gave food to every child at Lil' Man's table except him, which Mom and I always found suspicious. When the women proceeded to serve two more tables, Lil' Man deduced they weren't going to bring him any food. So, he reared back and, with a volume level that contradicted his three-year-old body, yelled, "Hey! One of you bitches, bring me my dinner!"

That was his first and last day at kindergarten.

Every time Son told the story, Mom and I said Lil Man's expulsion was shameful and the kindergarten should have cut him some slack. After all, everyone at the church, from the pastor to the kindergarten director, knew Lil' Man's grandfather and how he made his living. So, why not show some empathy and simply teach Lil' Man how to address women properly?

That's what we would have done because the child wasn't being disrespectful. He'd simply spoken to his teacher and her aide the way women were spoken to at his house. He hadn't known he was doing anything wrong.

It would have been so nice if those church folks—my mother's term for people who claim to be Christians but are judgmental or self-righteous—had simply explained that women weren't "bitches," told Lil' Man not to use that word again, and kept him as a student. Instead, they expelled him, blew the opportunity to keep a bright kid in school, and failed to aid a loving grandfather's quest to start a new chapter for his family.

Thankfully, Lil' Man's expulsion didn't end his school career. His grandfather found a more understanding kindergarten, which Lil' Man completed. He replicated that success throughout elementary school, high school and college. Lil' Man is now a corporate executive with a beautiful family, and society is one upstanding citizen richer—all because of a grandfather's determination to keep his grandson from becoming what was in the house.

Chapter Thirty-One

Watch for Hidden Toxicity in Good Homes

The "traditional" two-parent home is often placed upon a pedestal and described as "good." "Experts" and televangelists publicly voice their opinions on what a good home looks like. Comparison studies are conducted on the financial differences and sociological impacts across various family structures. Far too often, those opinions and studies produce an unfortunate result—the unjust vilification of single-parent and "nontraditional" homes.

In my experience, studies that favor nontraditional homes don't receive as much publicity as studies that vilify them. Consequently, some educators, social workers, et cetera, view two-parent homes as less problematic. As a result, signs of toxicity can be overlooked—much to the student's detriment.

Contrary to the aforementioned studies and opinions, I've found a family's toxicity level to be a much better indicator of a student's probability of success. Therefore, at Maranathan Academy, we keep our eyes peeled for signs of toxicity regardless of the family structure. The following three questions help us evaluate toxicity level:

1. Is the parent behaving in a manner that inspires respect, which motivates the child to behave? Or is the child allowed to see their parent engaging in activities that are illegal, unethical, or both—either of which can motivate the child to misbehave?
2. Can the parent express love, acceptance, and encouragement while lending a listening ear? Or is the child subjected to emotional or verbal abuse, judgmental replies, closed-minded advice, inflexible directives, or indifference?
3. Are consequences meted out to the child for inappropriate behavior? Or does the parent act as an enabler by making excuses for or encouraging inappropriate behavior?

Although two-parent homes are rare at Maranathan Academy, they present an equal or greater number of challenges than their nontraditional counterparts. In fact, some of my worst work experiences have come courtesy of parents and students from "good homes."

Tony

Antonio, who I nicknamed Tony, was the kind of person the world needs more of. He was funny, smart, ambitious, and filled with a desire to help people. That's how I, along with everyone else at Maranathan Academy, saw him. Unfortunately, our view wasn't universally shared.

Tony was gay, and a public school teacher had directed him to "display a more traditional preference" at an upcoming school dance for which Tony served on the planning committee. He ignored the directive and was promptly suspended and then expelled for "defiance of a school board employee and disruption of the learning environment." In other words, he refused to be apologetic about his sexuality and wouldn't pretend to be someone he wasn't. And I admired his honesty.

Tony was a videographer and did media broadcasts for churches across the city, including one pastored by his father, Reverend

Raymond Ingram. Despite the enrichment Tony's talent provided to his ministry, Rev. Ingram took every opportunity to persecute and belittle his son—saying he was going to "put a stop" to Tony's "sinfulness." He berated Tony's boyfriend so much that the young man stopped coming over. Tony's mom, Mrs. Ingram, never stood up for her son or herself. An area supervisor for a utility company, she was the family's primary breadwinner but was totally dominated by her husband. At his insistence, she ran several church auxiliaries, braved loneliness while he stayed out late with other ministers, and died a little each day as she watched the man she loved try to crush the spirit of the son she adored.

I suspected she was being abused but couldn't figure out how to broach the subject with her and offer my help.

"Can I come and live with one of you?" Tony asked one morning while I was talking with an instructor.

"What happened?"

"I've been trying to tough it out and keep living at home because of my mama. But if my daddy comes at me wrong one more time, I'm scared of what I might do. I'm tired of him calling me names every day, saying I make him sick!"

"Do you think your mom would come with you if you left?" I asked.

"I don't know, but she needs to. She's so lonely, and she's drinking more and more. Two weeks ago, my dad left to go on one of the retreats he takes with his friends. And three hours later, I found her passed out on the bed with a bottle of scotch. I'm really worried about her!"

"Well, Tony, if she's that lonely, why doesn't she just go with him sometimes?"

"Wives aren't allowed."

Uh-oh!

Tony was in such a state that the instructor and I asked him to come with us to the office and talk some more. As we walked, I began to think about his description of Rev. Ingram's behavior and mindset—trips with no wives allowed, constant persecution of

Tony, and an almost maniacal dislike of gay men. Things started to add up, and I knew I had to ask a question.

"Tony, has your father ever said anything about having dated men?"

"What? No! He hates gay men! That's why he hates me," exclaimed Tony, then shook his head and sighed.

"Well, my mother always said—and I've seen it play out this way many times—that the people who scream the loudest about hating gay people are often gay themselves and trying to hide it."

"No, Miss Dukes. My daddy couldn't even stand to be in the living room if me and my boyfriend were sitting next to each other on the couch. He said he didn't see how I could stand to be that close to a man, much less kiss one. No, he can't be gay."

"Tony," I said gently. "Some people use homophobic persecution to keep anyone from figuring out they're gay. We need to have a conference with him and your mom. Something's got to give about the way you're being treated."

The parent conference was scheduled, and three days later, I stood at my office desk and watched Rev. Ingram make his entrance. He walked slowly through the door wearing skintight pink pants, red snakeskin shoes, a red shirt unbuttoned almost to the navel, and perfectly applied makeup—foundation, brows, and flesh-colored lip gloss. His wife walked in behind him and stood quietly near my desk, while he examined several degrees and photographs on the walls. The crisis counselor was already in the office, so I sent for Tony and started the conference when he arrived.

"Rev. Ingram, Tony is one of the smartest, most talented young men to ever attend Maranathan. He's humble and brilliant and has a bright future. But I'm troubled. He seems unhappy and—"

"If he's unhappy, it's his own fault! He ought to stop being a [homophobic slur]!" interrupted his father. He then started on a rant that included scriptures, more homophobic slurs, and chastisement of me for letting Tony talk about "his sinfulness."

The vitriol that flowed from the lips of the "minister" had me wanting to take up a collection to help Tony and his mother rent an apartment and escape.

Only once during the rant did Mrs. Ingram try to speak.

"Tony is a good son, and uh—" She stopped suddenly, looking toward her husband.

I looked, too, and saw Rev. Ingram partially standing as he gave his wife a look that could have curdled milk, leaned threateningly toward her, and growled, "Shut up!"

Assuming the posture of someone preparing to take a blow, she did as she was told. It was textbook battered woman behavior and strengthened my suspicion that she was being abused.

With his wife silent once again, Rev. Ingram resumed his rant against Tony. "He's a [homophobic slur], and a [homophobic slur], and he's—"

"Honest!" I exclaimed. Silently, I was thinking that Tony's honesty about who he was and who he loved was likely the exact opposite of his father.

When Rev. Ingram turned to me to reply, I decided to poke the bear. "You do realize this is your child, right?"

He gasped and narrowed his eyes.

"Tony is a fantastic kid who does everything he can to make the world a better place. Lots of fathers would give anything to have a son like him, but not you. No, you mistreat and refuse to accept him instead of celebrating him having the courage to be who he is. As far as I'm concerned, he deserves a medal for not giving in to societal pressure to pretend to be someone he isn't. That's so much better than living on the down-low like so many of our Black men are doing. Don't you think?" I asked with a slightly raised eyebrow.

If looks could kill, I would have been dead.

"No! And, if he keeps on being a [homophobic slur], I'm going to put him out!" spat Rev. Ingram, quickly rising from his seat.

"If you keep verbally abusing him, I'm going to notify child protective services, and from the way you just spoke to your wife, I might call the police, too. Ask them to drive by and do a wellness check on her!" I said hotly, springing from my chair.

That got the good reverend's attention. As the saying goes, he "started acting like he had some act right."

"Now, Sister Dukes, there's no reason to do that. I'll stop talking to Antonio and his mother so rough and increase my prayers to have patience with them. Alright?" His voice was calm and filled with charm.

"Maybe so, maybe not. We'll have to see how you do. But I am going to pray for you to realize how blessed you are to have Tony and Mrs. Ingram in your life."

Obviously displeased with my reply, Rev. Ingram's newfound charm disappeared.

"And I'm going to pray for you to learn how to act! Somebody needs to make you understand a woman's place!" he snapped.

Not trusting my ability to remain civil, I ended the conference, told Tony to go back to class, and asked the crisis counselor to see the Ingrams out.

Less than a minute later, Mrs. Ingram returned.

"I told my husband I'd left my glasses in here, but I just needed to thank you for what you're doing to help my baby. I really appreciate you, Miss Dukes."

"You're more than welcome, Mrs. Ingram. I'd like to help with what you're going through with Rev. Ingram, too. When you get what my mom used to call your 'nuff of him,' let me know. I have several friends who love to help women escape abusive marriages."

"Yes, ma'am. I sure will," she said tearfully before turning to leave and rejoin her husband.

I was more concerned about her and Tony than ever and said a prayer for their strength and deliverance.

The conference resulted in an unspoken truce between Tony and his father, one which allowed genuine peace in the house for a few days. Then, an unexpected bout of conscience tore Tony's life apart and revealed deceit and illusion as major players in his family.

"My daddy is gay!" Tony yelled, bursting into my office.

"What happened?" I asked, looking up from my desk.

"He and Mama had an argument. She went to their room, and he came to mine, wanting to talk. He'd never done that before."

"What did he say?"

"That he understood me wanting to have sex with men because he has sex with men. But then he said I shouldn't let people know what I like to do. That I should do like him and put together a small group of men that only has sex with each other. That way, nobody finds out," he said, then sat down, shaking his head.

"Does your mom know?" I asked.

"Yes! And she's been letting him say all that stuff to me!"

Tony continued, confiding that his father told him the men in his minister's group were his "small group of men" and that their quarterly ministerial retreats were actually three-day orgies.

"All this time! My daddy's been gay all this time, and my mama knew it! And she let him treat me so bad! I can't believe this!" he exclaimed, then broke down in tears.

I let him cry it out, then called in our counselor. The three of us put our heads together and came up with some options, one of which involved Tony moving out and getting an apartment. Despite being hurt over her part in his father's deception, Tony balked at the idea of leaving his mom. The counselor and I acknowledged his concerns and pointed out he shouldn't sacrifice his right to be happy. Then, we helped him devise a way to still watch out for his mom.

Six weeks later, he graduated and enrolled in a computer training program. He and his boyfriend, who was studying to be a dental hygienist, leased an apartment and successfully completed their respective courses of study. They're both gainfully employed and blissfully happy with each other. Tony has a great life filled with friends and a few relatives who accept and uplift him.

Wonderful things happen when you help a child navigate how to escape from a toxic home.

Chapter Thirty-Two

Access and Sympathy: The Importance of Setting Boundaries

"Donna, can I invite Sharon to come over for Lily's birthday sleepover this weekend?" asked Leslie, who taught reading.

"And I want to invite the kids over for a barbecue at my house on Memorial Day," added Lisa, who taught art.

Sharon was a wonderful student who would gain much from getting out of the house over the weekend. And I sighed, dreading the response I was about to give. "I'm sorry, y'all, but no. Maranathan has a policy that prohibits students knowing where any of us live, remember?"

"I remember, but I was just hoping we could maybe make an exception this time," said Leslie, trailing off hopefully.

"I wish we could," came my fervent reply. I then reminded her of the policy's main purpose. It was designed to protect us from the retaliation of dismissed students and from students' families who sometimes see us as easy marks for money.

With a commiserating sigh, Leslie returned to her class. And I, for the umpteenth time, wished things could be the way they were in Maranathan's early years or even back in Mom's public school teaching days—a time when it was safe and somewhat commonplace for students to visit teachers at their homes.

Mom's students had a standing invitation to special church services, which were always followed by family dinners, all holiday dinners, and my birthday parties. Many kept in touch and told Mom how much they appreciated being included. They described the value those visits to our home added to their lives.

Wanting Maranathan to be just as or even more impactful on the lives of our students, I thought it only right to continue the practice. After all, decades of student visits had only produced one problem, which was very quickly solved. A boy whom Mom practically adopted stole her credit cards and bought things for his mother, friends, and himself. Mom canceled the cards and stopped mentoring him—no real harm done. Unfortunately, we would learn the hard way that letting students get too close can be dangerous.

Sarina

Sarina was from the islands, spoke in melodically beautiful but broken English, and was absolutely precious. She captured the hearts of everyone who met her. Her father had found work in America and left her in the care of relatives, who'd neglected her horribly. When Bembe, her father, learned of his daughter's mistreatment, he'd sent for Sarina. Since his job required constant travel, it was decided that she would live with his fiancée Helen, a former student of Mom's—which is how Maranathan Academy came into the picture.

The child was behind academically and had behavior problems. Helen called Mom, briefed her on the situation, and was encouraged to enroll Sarina immediately.

Determined for her to be emotionally compensated for all the mistreatment she'd suffered, Mom and I brought Sarina into our family. She was included in everything—trips to the mall, restaurant outings, and, to her great delight, holiday celebrations. She was placed on the Christmas lists of everyone in our immediate family, resulting in an avalanche of presents. Sarina blossomed under the attention, mastered English, and became an honor roll student.

Though proud of her progress, Mom and I were concerned about Sarina's mental health. She would sometimes freeze during class and stare into space, almost as if in a trance. Compliments from boys about her beauty triggered angry verbal outbursts. And the replies she gave when questioned about her behavior were just as disturbing as the behavior itself.

"I was thinking about when somebody set this man on fire, and we watched him burn." Or "I get mad when they say I'm pretty because they're lying! I'm not pretty! I'm ugly!"

We recommended counseling Sarina's soon-to-be stepmother. Helen rejected the idea, insisting the child was "strong enough" to handle problems on her own.

A few weeks later, Bembe was murdered. Sarina was inconsolable—hysterical one minute, plotting revenge against his killer the next. To make matters worse, her dad's family, whom she hadn't heard from in two years, insisted that Sarina return to the Islands.

As is common among abused children, Sarina still loved her relatives despite all the pain they'd caused her and found herself torn between returning to the family whose love she so desperately wanted or staying where she was safe and genuinely loved. It all proved to be too much—losing her father and being in the middle of a tug-of-war between his relatives and Helen. The trancelike episodes and angry outbursts against boys worsened. They became more frequent and expanded to include any boy who spoke to her, compliment or not.

Mom and I recommended counseling again. This time, Helen accepted the recommendation and signed documents granting permission for Sarina to start attending sessions. We rejoiced—too soon.

Days later, Helen learned Bembe's job benefits included a large life insurance policy of which Sarina was the sole beneficiary. Permission for the child to receive counseling was withdrawn. A relative had convinced Helen that the insurance company would not pay out on the policy if they learned Sarina was in counseling.

Despite our best efforts, Mom and I couldn't change Helen's mind. So, we continued to shower Sarina with attention and prayed for the best.

Unfortunately, one day, a boy asked to borrow some paper from Sarina, and she attacked him. We quickly pulled her off him but had to send her home and insist she be given a psychiatric evaluation. Helen refused and withdrew her from school. Two years later, we learned that Sarina had attempted to strangle Helen and had been admitted to the psychiatric ward of a local hospital for observation.

Six years after that, I discovered a young man walking down the side of our house to a car parked in our driveway. A now-adult Sarina exited the car and confronted me, claiming she didn't finish school because we "put her out." I explained that we hadn't. We'd only recommended she get counseling. I further explained that when she attacked that boy, we had no choice but to require her to get a psychiatric evaluation to return to school, but Helen had refused and chosen to withdraw her from us instead. I then offered her the opportunity to talk with Maranathan's counselor and apply for our adult education program.

"No, thanks. I just wanted to see if you still lived here," she replied, then left.

Two days later

"Jack! Donna! The house is on fire!" Son shouted.

The shout reached the backyard, where I sat with Mom as she sunned her legs to relieve swelling and arthritis pain. We entered the house as fast as we could and were confronted by nearly impenetrable black smoke billowing down the hallway. Son bravely tried to fight through it and find the source, but it was futile. The smoke made breathing impossible, and the three of us barely managed to get outside.

Thanks to having a cell phone in my pocket, I was able to dial 911. Feeling helpless while watching the flames devour the house, we joined hands and prayed. Suddenly, a window on the second floor

Access and Sympathy: The Importance of Setting Boundaries 209

shattered, and huge flames shot out just as we heard the welcome wail of fire truck sirens.

Later, a fire inspector arrived and determined the cause of the blaze—two Molotov cocktails. One had been thrown at our front door and the other into a second-story window—our prayer room window, to be exact. When we shared the room's purpose and that it contained family heirlooms, the inspector nodded and said the choice of the room meant the arsonist was "someone who knew you, knew what was in that room, and what those things meant to you."

"Do you have any enemies? Made anybody mad recently? Because this was done by somebody who wanted to hurt you bad. If you had been in your bedrooms, you'd never have made it out alive."

I caught my breath at his words and began to shiver with realization. Whoever set the blaze had wanted to do more than burn down our house.

They'd wanted to burn us to death along with it.

Everyone close to us knew our Sunday routine. Church, dinner, then sports on the family room TV for Son, and perusal of Sunday sales papers for Mom and me while catching up on soaps in one of our bedrooms. Mom's aching legs had helped save our lives.

Sarina's "visit" came to mind, and I shared it with the inspector, lamenting over not having a way to get a current address or phone number. His reply was both consoling and disheartening.

"Don't worry about it. I hate to tell you this, but since she has a history of mental illness, even if we find her, she probably won't get anything done to her except hospitalization, maybe."

As he turned away to start wrapping up his inspection, Mom, Son, and I began to realize some of the precious items we'd lost, such as Mom's family Bible with its record of births, deaths, and marriages, Son's license to preach and his ministerial ordination certificate both signed by his late mentor, an antique table that dated back to the 1800s and had belonged to one of Mom's favorite cousins, and my prized, near mint condition original hardback collection of the complete Nancy Drew series.

Soon, the inspector and firemen left, and our trio stood looking at our house. Too shocked to weep but not to thank God for sparing our lives. We joined hands once again and prayed, so grateful to still have each other.

Months later, while sitting in a shopping mall food court, we encountered Sarina and her boyfriend.

Wearing a wide smile, she called out to us and began walking toward our table, her boyfriend in tow. As they approached, we hastily crafted a plan. When the couple reached us, Son would excuse himself to "go to the restroom," which really meant he'd alert a security guard and call the police.

It almost worked.

I asked for and received Sarina's number under the guise of wanting to keep in touch. Then Mom said she wanted to "catch up" and took the lead. She asked Sarina what she'd been up to.

"Not much, but what about y'all?" she asked with a small smirk.

Mom made some small talk about a past vacation and then mentioned the fire. A slow, sinister smile spread across Sarina's face.

"I bet y'all was crying, especially Donna! I bet she was crying and crying, wasn't she?" she asked. Her face was disturbingly alight with pleasure at the thought of my pain.

"No," Mom replied, "we were in shock. But I'm sure we would have cried if the house had burned down."

An angry scowl replaced Sarina's joyous expression.

"What do you mean? You still got the house? It didn't burn down?!"

Mom answered, "No, it didn't." Then she added, "And it's a miracle, too. Because someone threw a Molotov cocktail through the window!"

"They threw it in your upper room?" asked Sarina's boyfriend, who, to our knowledge, had never been inside our house.

Before Mom could answer, Sarina slapped his arm and stood.

"Shut up! We got to go!"

The two made a hasty retreat just moments before Son arrived with a security guard. I shared the phone number Sarina had given us with the police and the fire inspector, but it turned out to be bogus.

The entire incident forced me to face a sobering fact—unchecked sympathy for Sarina had left us vulnerable to harm. Our efforts to heal Sarina's past hurts had given her too much access to our lives and provided the perfect way for her to hurt us. So, I made a hard decision. Sympathy would be kept in check, and strict boundaries would be set for students. No matter what. It's painful, but Sarina taught me that not doing so hurts even worse.

Chapter Thirty-Three

Recharge, Reminisce, and Relish

While working on the front lines of the CAW, three Rs will see you through unavoidably tough times. It's not a matter of if you'll encounter tough times. It's only a matter of when. Thankless days, long hours, or being told to f*** off by someone you've done everything in your power to help will occur. If you haven't already done so, make the three R's a part of your routine—recharge, reminisce, and relish.

Recharge

A high level of motivation is crucial for a successful career in the CAW. But it is difficult to maintain, particularly when exhausted. If you're like me, you tend to put others first, ignore signs of fatigue, and fail miserably at scheduling time for self-care. For example, I had been running Maranathan for twenty-five years before I took a trip that didn't involve work, a family reunion, or a funeral.

Don't do that!

I believe that all CAW workers benefit from prioritizing self-care. Understanding the importance of making self-care a priority is helped by incorporating two questions posed by noted psychologists and authors Thomas Skovholt and Michelle Trotter-Mathison in their phenomenal book *The Resilient Practitioner: Burnout and*

Compassion Fatigue Prevention and *Self-Care Strategies for the Helping Professions*. These two questions are, "How do those in the caring professions, who use their own self as a method of change, prevent burnout and maintain professional vitality? How does one establish balance between other-care and self-care?"

The referenced questions helped me realize that we CAW workers must make sure "me time" is a fixture in our schedules so that we can recharge. If carving out time for yourself seems impossible, consider this statement from psychologist Jensen Reiser: "Selfcare builds resilience against stress. We can't control many of the stressors in our lives, so we must find ways to move through them with our health and wellness intact. How well we do that depends on how we practice caring for ourselves. Because taking care of yourself lowers stress, it acts as a protective barrier against burnout." If you decide to allow self-care time into your life and it resonates with you, feel free to make use of a three-statement mantra I use to feel less guilty about taking time out for myself:

1. It's okay to take a moment to relax. My mental, spiritual, and physical health are important.
2. Work passion and dedication should not result in self-neglect.
3. If I work myself to sickness or death, who will help my students, clients, family members, or others?

Reminisce

Several things can help get you through hard days, such as inviting former students to serve as speakers or looking through old photos and posts. For me, none is more effective than an informal gathering to take a trip down memory lane.

I love having mini Maranathan reunions, where grads return with their partners, spouses, and kids to take photos, make videos, and catch up. There's something magical in knowing that Maranathan played a part in their ability to have senior photos and family portraits instead of mugshots or being cover photos for obituary programs. Each reunion sparks recollections of when kids' "you-owe-me-something" attitudes disappeared and were replaced with rediscovered childlike innocence, which led to the making of really sweet, funny moments—like a hard-core gang kid trying to outrun his classmates to find the golden egg at an Easter egg hunt. Believe me, you have not lived until you've seen a six-foot-four-inch former gang member with "Rest-in-Peace-Memaw" tattooed on his neck, walking around munching on a chocolate bunny! You have not lived!

Relish

Because CAW-frontline work is so fast-paced, a new crisis often emerges before a current one can be dealt with. It's easy to short yourself when savoring victories, but try not to. Savoring current achievements provides the fuel needed to go toe to toe with new crises—at least, that's what it always does for me.

Quintavious

One day recently, Maranathan was its usual beehive of activity, with students bustling around to set up for our weekly art class. Watching from my office door, I spotted Quintavious, a gangly middle schooler, stealthily approaching an array of paint jars with a mischievous look on his face.

"Q, what are you doing?"

He startled and turned, his expression suddenly the picture of innocence as he said, "Nothing, Miss Dukes. I'm just being helpful and getting some paint to take to Sterling."

Ah-ha! The same Sterling Q had tricked into putting Tabasco sauce in his bowl of chili to see how many bottles of water Sterling would have to drink to "put out the fire."

"Was he going to be using the paint or wearing the paint you were taking him?" I asked with an arched eyebrow.

"How did you know?" Q gasped, then almost doubled over laughing.

When he caught his breath, he conceded, "Alright, Miss Dukes. I won't take him any paint."

"Thank you, Q. And I'm sure if he knew what you'd been planning, Sterling would thank you, too."

Despite being our resident prankster, Q was a constant source of motivation for everyone on staff. He had been expelled from public school for repeated episodes of violence and had come a long way in his very short time at Maranathan. He was one of three boys born to troubled parents. His mother suffered from abandonment and selfesteem issues, and his father, despite several stints in prison for dealing drugs, regularly told Q and his little brothers that he expected them to "expand the family business," which meant helping him to sell drugs.

Enrolling at Maranathan provided Q with access to adolescent crisis counseling, classes in anger management, and yoga. Soon, he and his schoolmates will be taking a mindfulness class—thanks to training received by staff when Maranathan was chosen to partner with the University of Alabama at Birmingham (UAB) on a grant. Our academic course of study and successful interventions led by credentialed counselors provide Q with the tools needed to succeed. He has left behind the mistakes of his past and, while facing challenges in the present, has earned two positions of responsibility—Maranathan Academy Ambassador and Youth Assistant to the Compliance Officer. Victories like Q's keep me going.

So, that's it—a career in the critically at-risk world, in a nutshell. Whatever route you decide to take, be it a finite time of volunteer or paid service, a career length commitment, or financial support, congratulate yourself for having a passion for helping your fellow humans.

If, by chance, you commit your life's work to front-line service in the CAW, please allow me to say, "Welcome!" It's not an easy path, but it will give you some of the most rewarding experiences of your life.

Epilogue

"Miss Dukes! The game is ready. Come on!" Weekly gaming time is given to every student who is up to date on assignments and has no dress code or behavioral violations.

The academic year is about to wrap up. And, despite significant and, at times, heartbreaking struggles dealt with by the majority of our students, great strides are being made every day. I don't know God's plans for their lives or problems, and that's okay. My faith tells me things will work out for those who stay the course. And that's enough. It's enough to know that at Maranathan, they have found hope, a second chance, and opportunities to grow. Here, they're free—to laugh, live, love, and learn how to dream.

Heading out of my office, I stop and smile. All the students have gathered to watch the game and egg on the players with good-natured trash talk. I'm one of the players and my name is being called in earnest.

"Here I come. Now, who am I playing?"

"Me!" declares DeAngelo, a relatively new student on probation for stealing a car.

"Congratulations, D! Let's see how fast I can win this game!" Big grins and howls of laughter greet my statement. Their laughter makes me stop again. And I take a moment to just look at my "babies" and revel over seeing smiles where there were frowns, hearing giggles instead of sobs, and being watched by eyes that shine with the light of hope instead of being dark with anger or despair.

I can hardly wait to see how their stories unfold.

References

Asante-Muhammad, D., Collins, C., Hoxie, J., & Nieves, E. (2016). (rep.). *The Ever-Growing GAP: Without Change, African-American and Latino Families Won't Match White Wealth for Centuries* (pp. 1–32). Washington, D. C.: Institute for Policy Studies.

Bennett, L. (2007). *Before the Mayflower: A history of Black America*. Johnson.

Best Books. *Complete Bible Reference Study (4 in 1) King James Version Bible with Strongs markup*. (2015). Best Books.

Bor, J., Venkataramani, A. S., Williams, D. R., & Tsai, A. C. (2018). Police killings and their spillover effects on the mental health of black Americans: a population-based, quasi-experimental study. *The Lancet, 392*(10144), 302-310.

Brooks, G. (2006). *The Essential Gwendolyn Brooks* (E. Alexander, Ed.). Library of America.

Brown, R. (2010, March 31). Jaime Escalante's legacy, in and out of the classroom. The Atlantic. https://www.theatlantic.com/entertainment/archive/2010/03/jaime-escalantes-legacy-in-and-out-of-the-classroom/38263/

Carson, E. A., & Kluckow, R., Office of Justice Programs, Prisoners in 2022 – Statistical Tables 1–48 (2023). D.C., Washington; U.S. Department of Justice. Retrieved 2024, https://bjs.ojp.gov/document/p22st.pdf

Collins, K., Connors, K., Davis, S., Donohue, A., Gardner, S., Goldblatt, E., Hayward, A., Kiser, L., Strieder, F. Thompson, E. (2010). *Understanding the impact of trauma and urban poverty on family systems: Risks, resilience, and interventions.* Baltimore, MD: Family Informed Trauma Treatment Center. http://nctsn.org/nccts/nav.do?pid=ctr_rsch_prod_ar or http://fittcenter.umaryland.edu/WhitePaper.aspx

Dolan, E. W. (2024, March). *The startling impact of early life adversity revealed in new neuroscience research.* PsychPost. https:// www. https://www.psypost.org/the-startling-impact-of-early-life-adversity-revealed-in-new-neuroscience-research/

Dukes, D. (2016, April 6). *Let's Address the Needs of Critically At-Risk Youth | Donna Dukes | TEDxBirmingham*. YouTube. https://www.youtube.com/watch?v=T1_DJh10Mgs

Dylan, J. (2022, February 12). A NLV police officer responded to a homicide. Then he made a life-changing decision. Review Journal. https://www.reviewjournal.com/crime/a-nlv-police-officer-responded-to-a-homicide-then-he-made-a-life-changing-decision-2527841/

Gollub, E., Green, J., Richardson, L., Kaplan, I., & Shervington, D. (2019). Indirect violence exposure and mental health symptoms among an urban public-school population: Prevalence and correlates. PLoS ONE 14(11): e0224499. https://doi.org/10.1371/journal.pone.0224499

Kübler-Ross, E., & Byock, I. (2019). *On death & dying: What the dying have to teach doctors, nurses, clergy & their own families.* Scribner.

Levin, P. (Director). (1981). The Marva Collins Story [Film]. Hallmark Hall of Fame.

Maslow, A. H. (2011). *Hierarchy of needs: A theory of human motivation.* All About Psychology.

Okoye, C. (2008). *Mary McLeod Bethune: Words of wisdom.* Author House.

Poetry House. (2020). *150 most famous poems: Emily Dickinson, Robert Frost, William Shakespeare, Edgar Allan Poe, Walt Whitman and many more.*

Reiser, J. (n.d.). *Nurturing Well-being: Why Prioritizing Self-Care Is Essential.* Lyra. 2023, https://www.lyrahealth.com/blog/self-care/

Ross, K. M., Sullivan, T., O'Connor, K., Hitti, S., & Leiva, M. N. (2021). A community specific framework of risk factors for youth violence: A qualitative comparison of community stakeholder perspectives in a low income, urban community. *Journal of Community Psychology*, 49(5), 1134–1152. https://doi.org/10.1002/jcop.22497

Rutter, M. (2016). Why is the topic of the biological embedding of experiences important for translation?. *Development and Psychopathology*, 28(4pt2), 1245-1258.

Slaughter, R. (2009, February 11). *Marva Collins speaks*. Issuu. https://issuu.com/rslaughter/docs/marva_collins_interview

Smith Lee, J. R., & Robinson, M. A. (2019). "That's my number one fear in life. It's the police": Examining young Black men's exposures to trauma and loss resulting from police violence and police killings. *Journal of Black Psychology*, 45(3), 143-184.

Soltis, A. (2013, September 1). *"bored" teens accused of killing jogger were arrested after threatening to murder 17-year-old, cops say*. New York Post. https://nypost.com/2013/08/22/bored-teens-accused-of-killing-jogger-were-arrested-after-threatening-to-murder-17-year-old-cops-say/

Torrats-Espinosa, G. (2020). Crime and inequality in academic achievement across school districts in the United States. *Demography*, 57(1), 123-145.

Skovholt, T. M., & Trotter-Mathison, M. (2016). *The resilient practitioner: Burnout and Compassion Fatigue Prevention and self-care strategies for the helping professions.* Routledge, Taylor & Francis Group.

Whittaker, C., Qubein, N. R., & Rosasco, R. J. (2021). *Eleanor Roosevelt & Mary McLeod Bethune: An unusual friendship*. Advance Civility Press, LLC.

Acknowledgments

I am a firm believer that certain people act as catalysts for the accomplishment of goals. To that end, it is with profound gratitude that I acknowledge—

My late grandparents, Isaac and Lena Bates and Sarah Dukes Coleman, respectively. Although the need to work and help take care of siblings made it necessary for them to drop out of school, all three had a deep love for education, devoured books of poetry and literary classics, and made sure each of their children graduated from college and, in many cases, earned postgraduate degrees.

My parents, Frank and Jacquelyn Dukes, for constantly encouraging me, celebrating all academic and developmental milestones, and showing me the importance of concern for others. On a sad and indescribably painful note, I must acknowledge the loss of "Son," my father, Reverend Frank Dukes, who made his Heavenly transition on November 11, 2023 (Veteran's Day).

Dr. Thad James, Jr. and Bishop Levoid Trimble for invaluable scriptural consultation and enrichment.

Authors Andre Beaupre, T.K. Thorne, and Frank White, who generously shared insights and encouragement throughout this process.

Erica T, Ernest B, Eva B, Ginger F, Hunter T, Ida D, Kimberly O, Laura P, Leslie K, Lisa O, Ryan C, Susan S, and Bishop Marie T, for wonderful read-throughs, feedback, prayers, and good vibes.

My Aunt/Godmother Gwendolyn Patricia Oden (Pat) and my sister Tammy Doerner (who has been my sister since the day she enrolled in my mom's ninth-grade science class and declared my mother was going to be her mother too), I'm beyond grateful for receiving fantastic critiques, much needed "just checking on you" memes and well-timed calls from my nieces, who provided hilarious updates on their pre-K and kindergarten classes.

Arrelia Callins, treasured, icon of southern hospitality, legendary cashier, and mentor, for being an inexhaustible source of wisdom and encouragement, continuing to selflessly serve as a surrogate grandmother for any Maranathan Academy student in need of one and for helping to raise scholarships that get kids off the street and into the Academy's classrooms—bless you! You're an angel!

Teachers and administrators who played key roles in my formative education, my elementary school principals, the renowned educators Dr. Margaret B. Little and Dr. Rosa P. Hanks, and role models of fashion savvy, empathy, and firmness. Allene Avery, Vernora Patterson, and Kathy York for imparting the importance of utilizing different teaching styles to fit the unique needs of students.

The wonderful scholarship and program-sustaining donors; hard-working, dedicated faculty, staff, and volunteers; amazing alumni; precious enrolled students; and all involved parents and guardians of Maranathan Academy.

Last but certainly not least —

My editors, Amy Pattee Colvin and T.K. Thorne.

The amazing Chris Jones for magnanimously lending his genius as Phase III copy editor.

The ever-patient Anna Hartzog and Lauren Gentry of Village Editorial for the incredible final phase of copy editing.

The phenomenal folks at Rocky Heights Print & Binding.

Thanks to everyone for being such blessings in my life!

I appreciate you!

About the Author

Donna Dukes, Founder and Executive Director of Maranathan Academy, was born and raised in Birmingham, Alabama. She holds a Bachelor of Arts in Political Science from Miles College, where she graduated valedictorian with summa cum laude honors in 1991, a graduate certificate in nonprofit management from Harvard University, and a Master of Liberal Arts in Management from Harvard University.

On September 3, 1991, Donna founded Maranathan Family Learning Center and Academy (MFLC&A), a 501(c)(3) nonprofit alternative school and learning center for critically at-risk youth and adult students. Its primary goal is to break intergenerational, cyclical dependency on government assistance in the critically at-risk populace.

Over the last thirty-two years, MFLC&A (Maranathan Academy) has positively affected over 2,000 lives and graduated nearly 400 students. It is the only school in Birmingham, Alabama, that works exclusively with critically at-risk students and the only private school in Birmingham willing to accept students expelled for weapons-related or violent offenses.

Donna is a Telly Award-winning filmmaker, a TEDx speaker, and a highly sought-after presenter. She credits her success to being blessed with great parents who taught her the importance of a strong work ethic, academic excellence, and faith.

In recognition of the tremendous impact of her work at Maranathan Academy, Donna was inducted into the Martin Luther King, Jr. International College of Ministers and Laity at Morehouse College; named a Woman to Watch by the Birmingham Business Journal; received the Brother Bryan Prayer Point Award from the Women's Committee of 100 for Birmingham; was named a Regional Community Leader by national jeweler Kendra Scott; and was presented with an Outstanding Community Contributor award by the Alabama Chapter of the National Organization of Black Law Enforcement Executives (NOBLE).

Donna is a member of Sixth Avenue Baptist Church, Birmingham East Kiwanis Club, the Women's Committee of 100 for Birmingham, and serves on the Board of Directors of the Women's Committee of 100 for Birmingham.

She enjoys public speaking, cooking, reading, listening to a variety of music genres, and going to the movies (action movies are her favorite) and the theater.

Donna works tirelessly to bring the plight of critically at-risk students to the attention of the public and private sectors and to ensure that her students embrace academic opportunities, discard victim mentalities, practice inclusion, accept personal responsibility for their actions, and become productive, contributing members of society.

About the Author

Thanks so much for reading *This Way to Hope: The Challenges, Hard Truths, and Triumphs of Working with Critically At-Risk Students!*

Please learn more about the Critically At-Risk World (CAW), Maranathan Academy, This Way to Hope's author Donna Dukes by visiting the websites or scanning the QR Codes provided below:

Donna Dukes' TEDx Talk
www.youtube.com/watch?v=T1_DJh10Mgs&t=29s

Website of Maranathan Academy
www.maranathanac.org

Donne Dukes' Website
www.donnadukes.com

STAND! Untold Stories from the Civil Rights Movement
www.standthedocumentary.com

www.ingramcontent.com/pod-product-compliance
Lightning Source LLC
Chambersburg PA
CBHW020537030426
42337CB00013B/882